West Country Verses
Edited by Claire Tupholme

 Young**Writers**

First published in Great Britain in 2008 by:
Young Writers
Remus House
Coltsfoot Drive
Peterborough
PE2 9JX
Telephone: 01733 890066
Website: www.youngwriters.co.uk

SB ISBN 978-1 84431 469 0

Foreword

Young Writers was established in 1991 and has been passionately devoted to the promotion of reading and writing in children and young adults ever since. The quest continues today. Young Writers remains as committed to the nurturing of poetic and literary talent as ever.

This year's Young Writers competition has proven as vibrant and dynamic as ever and we are delighted to present a showcase of the best poetry from across the UK and in some cases overseas. Each poem has been selected from a wealth of *Little Laureates* entries before ultimately being published in this, our sixteenth primary school poetry series.

Once again, we have been supremely impressed by the overall quality of the entries we have received. The imagination, energy and creativity which has gone into each young writer's entry made choosing the poems a challenging and often difficult but ultimately hugely rewarding task - the general high standard of the work submitted ensured this opportunity to bring their poetry to a larger appreciative audience.

We sincerely hope you are pleased with this final collection and that you will enjoy *Little Laureates West Country Verses* for many years to come.

Contents

Joe Hewitt-Long (11)	45
Chloë Cunningham (10)	46
Matthew Barrington (10)	46
Poppy Selman (10)	47
Adam Frampton (10)	47
Jasmin Barber (11)	48
Sophie Hanks (10)	48
Amy Dolman (10)	49
Edward Sawyer (10)	49
Alice Richards (11)	50
Kane Fernandez (10)	50
Katherine Sawyer (10)	51
Jesse Gibbs (11)	51
Charlotte Brown (10)	52
Krystina Clark (10)	52
Charlotte Sawyer (10)	53
Georgina Dalton (10)	53
Jessica Fuller (10)	54
Arren Roach (10)	54
Kathryn Damoglou Pugh (11)	55
Chloe Sheppard (10)	55
Chloe Jagger (10)	56
Neil Knight (10)	56
Tuesday Blade Jeffries (10)	57
Dominic Biddle (10)	57
Josh Scott (10)	57

Kingswood Primary School, Wotton-under-Edge

Eloise McAllister (10)	58
Freya Ball (10)	59
Victoria Copeland (10)	60
Chloe Moss (9)	60
Jennifer Smith (10)	60

Longlevens Junior School, Longlevens

Kathryn Price (10)	61
Alice Loveday (10)	61
Sarah Milne (10)	61
Laura Thomas (10)	61
Georgina Parry (10)	62
Jack Hughes (10)	62

George Tirel (10)	62
Muazin Asad (10)	62
Alexander Bates (10)	63
Elizabeth Willett (10)	63
Dominic Trott (10)	63
Harry Bevins (11)	63
Toby Lawrence (11)	64
Robert Grainger (10)	64
Emma Cahill (10)	64
Molly Geddes (10)	64
Kieran Hayward (10)	65
Sam Gabb (11)	65
Joe Richardson (10)	65
Danny McCarthy (10)	65
Megan Hunt (8)	66

Manor Court Primary School, Chard

Matthew Lacey (9)	66
Jessica Kelly (9)	67
Sophie Baker (10)	67
Tiffany Watson (10)	67
Tilly Porthouse (9)	68
Katherine Hall-Roberts (9)	68
Kelsey Skinner (9)	68
Jake Crump (9)	69
Kirsty McQueen (9)	69
Rheannon Payne (10)	69
Tianna Swain (10)	70
Daniel Brown (9)	70
Samuel Hall (9)	70
Charlene Pablo (10)	71
Ellis Lewis (9)	71
Liam Willcocks (9)	71
Mary Smith (10)	72
Laura Watts (10)	72
Amy Blanksby (10)	72
Alfie Arnold (10)	73
Daniel Mason (10)	73
Shannon Clark (10)	73
Christopher Goodhew (10)	74
Jordi Morgan (10)	74

Matthew Hill (10)	74
Daniel Lee Smith (11)	75
Shannon Baker (10)	75
Connor Morgan (10)	75
Laura Hall (10)	76
Amy Laura Gage (11)	76
Christopher Haughton (10)	76
Hannah Pearce (10)	77
Jordan Totterdell (10)	77
Ashley Briant (10)	77
Wednesday Watson (11)	78
Warren Lewis (10)	78
Alice Fenner (10)	78
Alana Hake (8)	79
Louise Mackenzie (10)	79
Jess Mathieson (10)	79
Sophie Holloway (11)	80
Zoe Molesworth (9)	80
Niamh Rodgers (8)	80
Tyrone Payne (8)	81
Amy Barrett (8)	81
Ben James Grime (10)	81
Tony Redman (10)	82
Leonel Cruz (8)	82
Sophie White (10)	82
Lewis Day (8)	82
Cristine Pablo (8)	83
Abigail Trott (8)	83
Fraser Porthouse (8)	83
Jack Cruise (9)	83
Kira Bellamy (8)	84
Neil Parkes (9)	84
Jake Ripley (8)	84
Liam Clark (9)	84
Chloe Rendell (8)	85
Kelly Burke (8)	85
Adam Walker (8)	85
Phoebe Earl (9)	85
Dominic Lane (8)	86
James Parsons (8)	86
Kate Hall (8)	86
Lucy Bailey (8)	87

Josh Totterdell (9)	87
Caitlin Grime (8)	87
Mollie Briant (9)	88
Abbie Thompson (9)	88
Savanna Hall (10)	88
Tiffany Zenda (9)	89
Alice Hall (9)	89
Daniel Da Silva (9)	89
Kylie Jeynes (9)	90
Hannah Lord (9)	90
Courtney Wyatt (9)	90
Leanne Grimstead (9)	91
Mae Daniels (9)	91
Emily Bilboe (8)	91
Rebecca Orchard (9)	92
Kirsty Robertson (9)	92
Rhyann Watton (9)	92
James Woodcraft (8)	93
Ryan Board (9)	93
Liam Board (9)	93
Megan Curtis (9)	94
Elise Bradley (9)	94
Emily Boyland (9)	94
Charlotte Davies (9)	95
Rebecca Black (9)	95
Vicky Matthews (8)	95
Harry Meggitt (10)	96
Kirsty Rendell (10)	96

Walton Primary School, Walton

Matthew Long (9)	96
Erin McKenzie (9)	97
Alina Briscomb (9)	97
Bethany Reece (9)	97
Georgina Buckner (10)	98
Francesca Fallows (10)	98
Charlotte Dearman (10)	99
Jay Daniells (8)	99
Sophie Purchase (9)	100
Sam Vowles (10)	100
Chloe Dykes (10)	100

Karla White (10)	101
Alfred Beaty (9)	101
Lauren Baker (9)	101
Hannah Toal (9)	102
Katherine Hubbuck (10)	102
Abbie Robins (10)	102
Izzy Hicks (10)	103
Olivia Nelson (9)	103
Daisy Huxter (10)	103
Georgia Corrigan (10)	104
Charlie France (10)	105
Chloe Pitman (8)	105
Grace Hegarty (8)	106
Abigail Lockyer (9)	106
Francesca Chinnock (10)	107
Liberty Bingham (10)	107
Hannah Corrigan (9)	108
Katherine Fallows (9)	108
Megan Bratcher (8)	108
Charlotte Peach (9)	109
Lauren Kite (8)	109
Melissa Brandon (8)	109
Thomas Fallows (8)	110
Samuel Chant (8)	110
Fiona Shirley (9)	110

Wansdyke Primary School, Whitchurch

Chadley Tolliver (11)	111
Casey Bardsley (10)	111
Charlie Lenehan (8)	111
Carlia Zographos (10)	112
Callum Matthews (10)	112
Sophie Shaw (8)	113
Thomas Shorland (8)	113
Paula Pomothy (11)	114
Chelsea Harrison (10)	115
Dan Bartley (11)	116
Molly Selby (10)	116
Tom Martin (10)	117
James Ford	117
Aimee Coombs (10)	118

The Poems

Ice Skating

One day I went ice skating,
It was a bundle of fun,
Way better than any dating,
The ice was gleaming like the sun.

I went with my mates,
Who helped me put on my skates,
When on the ice, Giles was the master,
Then after I had some pasta.

Jack Lockey (9)
Andoversford Primary School, Cheltenham

Soldier

Soldiers secure secrets
Soldiers save lives
Soldiers secure nations
Soldiers fight for England
Soldiers don't give up
Soldiers risk their lives like a protective pack of wolves
Soldiers sometimes die
Soldiers sometimes lie
Soldiers write poems, like I am doing now
Soldiers win the war (sometimes).

Freddie Nelson (9)
Avondale School, Bulford

My War Inspiration

Fear is like poverty coming towards you at an
amazingly fast speed.
Where war is at your doorstep waiting to be picked up.
Fear is like letting your passion rot away in poppy fields.
Fear is nothing but pain and frustration.
Fear is like one day everything is normal and the next day,
bang! War.
Fear finds you and makes you scared of your shadow.
Fear is like wind swirling towards you.
Your fear catches you out as you nervously walk
towards the battlefield.
Your fear may be a success or not.

Isabel Smith (9)
Avondale School, Bulford

Fear

Fear is like waiting to hear orders for war.
Fear is like war coming, coming towards you, but you can't stop it.
Fear is like war, never-ending and you never know when it stops.
Fear is like nothing, nobody in an enormous field.
Fear is like soldiers, secrets, words unheard.
Fear is like listening to people dying, fighting.
Fear is like lightning bolts everywhere but you don't know
where to go.
Fear is everywhere, sometimes you don't know you've got it,
but everybody has.

Nathan Banham (9)
Avondale School, Bulford

Hope

Hope is like changing fate for the most in need of luck.
Hope is for a fighter carrying our future on his back.
Hope is the luck for victory, for a great fight.
Hope is needed for war, for the helpless for the world.
Hope is for hungry people, who have nothing, who are unlucky.
Hope is not impenetrable and not always successful
                                            but can be forceful.
Hope is an extra chance to win a war.
Hope is everything to a soldier.

Rufus Redwood-Rowe (9)
Avondale School, Bulford

Silence

Silence is like a soldier in a cellar strapped to a post.
Silence is like nothing.
Silence is like nobody is around you.
Silence is like after a bomb has hit your city.
Silence is like everybody fast asleep in bed tucked up.
Silence is like an amazing star way up in the sky.
Silence is like a shot soldier.

Taylor Clarke (9)
Avondale School, Bulford

Hailstone

Hailstone shoots like a bullet
but stares like an eye.
Screaming and yelling
on the way down to the ground,
reminds me of an army man.

Joe Lewis (10)
Berry Hill CP School, Coleford

The Moon's Stages

The full moon is like a letter O with a middle stuck in.
Like a disco ball sparkling while it rotates.
Like a marble being rolled into space by a naughty child.

The changing moon is like a chocolate cake being eaten gradually.
Like an onion being peeled carefully.
Like an orange being peeled and eaten, segment by segment.

The crescent moon is like a white door handle to the
                                          pleasant day ahead.
Like a hammock with someone falling asleep, ready to
                                          sleep the night away.
Like a letter C, the third letter of the alphabet.

Dorothy Giles (9)
Berry Hill CP School, Coleford

The Lightning Monster

The lightning dances crazily in the air,
Hypnotising people from its stare.

Grabs its prey from the sky,
Puts it in its mouth way up high.

He sings opera badly,
Because he caught his prey gladly.

Now he says, 'I'm not hungry anymore,
I'm just thirsty so I want some more,
Ha, ha, ha, ha!'

Kristina Gray (10)
Berry Hill CP School, Coleford

The Wicked Moon Poem

The full moon is like a disco ball spinning in the darkness.
Like a pearl just opened from the dark.
Like a white light flying through space.

The changing moon is like a pizza being sliced.
Like a chocolate cake being eaten.
Like a banana ready to eat.

The crescent moon is like a big happy smile.
Like a tree being pushed by the wind.
Like a letter C in the alphabet.

Sam Jessop (8)
Berry Hill CP School, Coleford

The Moon

The full moon is like a disco ball lighting up the sky.
Like a round sphere spinning around.
Like a cheesy pizza, steamy hot.

The changing moon is like an apple slowly being eaten.
Like a balloon going down.
Like a chocolate cake sponge nibbled by a naughty child.

The crescent moon is like a piece of melon.
Like a banana ready to be peeled.
Like a big grin from a cheeky child.

Zoe Ho (8)
Berry Hill CP School, Coleford

The Rain And Snow Night Out

The snow whispered to the rain,
'Let's go and cause some trouble tonight!'

They jogged to a nearby bus stop
And hitched a lift to the bowling alley and KFC.

Because the snowball lost 4 points
He began to cry puddles of water.

So the rain began to cry with joy
As the snowball began to roll down the alley!

Charlie Goble (10)
Berry Hill CP School, Coleford

Thunder

The thunder comes running to the land.
It bangs like size 99 professional drums.
It crashes and bangs in the atmosphere
and deafens people and then moves on.

Reece Williams (10)
Berry Hill CP School, Coleford

Hailstones

The hail attacks,
The glass shatters.

Tapping on tables,
Jumps away
But will be back another day.

Alex Watkins (10)
Berry Hill CP School, Coleford

Lightning

Sharp flashing knives
shoot to the ground.
It clashes below,
scanning for trees.

It roars as it zaps
through the sky.

Lightning.

Liam Morgan (10)
Berry Hill CP School, Coleford

The Snowball

There once was a snowball
Who was dancing and singing
But when a child came and picked it up
It began crying with laughter.

Kaleigh Pritchard (10)
Berry Hill CP School, Coleford

Snow

Snow arrives by
walking through the air.

It sleeps quietly
in a big white bed,
then it wakes up
and slowly drifts away.

Megan Giles (10)
Berry Hill CP School, Coleford

The Forest And The Wolf

The forest is like a howling wolf
Big, scary and creepy

Trees are reaching for sunlight
Like a wolf's fuzzy belly

At night the stars are like the wolf's beady eyes
Gazing down at you

Wetness of the leaves is like the nose of the wolf
The forest is a scary place

People who go into the forest
may not come out!

**Jasmine Baker (11), Georgia Fieldhouse
& Milly Templeton-Browne (10)**
Christ Church Primary School, Weston-super-Mare

Illusions

The rainbow is my vision,
The waterfalls are my tears,
Waiting to flood my face,
The sun is my thoughts,
The moon is my fear,
Which terrifies me,
The mist is my feelings,
The wind is my breath,
Which is cold and damp,
These are the illusions of my life.

Isabelle Jeffrey, Jennifer Kuht & Rebecca Capel (10)
Christ Church Primary School, Weston-super-Mare

Forest

The forest rumbles
And the trees sway
They could be like us one day
The big crowd pushing and shoving every day
What do they say?

The wavy branches fell on the floor
Did they do anything more?
The woodpecker pecked the trees
And there was a great breeze.

Courtney Radford, Hannah Williams & May Barnett (10)
Christ Church Primary School, Weston-super-Mare

Sunset

I swoop down below
My colours spreading across the sky
I settle down on the sea, low, low, low.

I repeat, I repeat what I do every night
I do not fly at dawn
I do not fly at night
For I am the parrot of the sunlight.

Emily Fraser & Nicole Hofgartner (11)
Christ Church Primary School, Weston-super-Mare

Hate

Hate is red like a soiled heart which made me stay up
through the night and it's quite a fright.
It sounds like a heart breaking into little pieces.
It tastes like a rotten apple from a tree.
It smells like a rotten egg.
It looks like a monster from Hell that's invisible.
It feels like a pointed rock.
It reminds me of freezing snow when you can't go out and play.

Leon Hayward (9)
Christ Church Primary School, Weston-super-Mare

Laughter

Laughter is like a yellow sun, filled with fun.
It reminds me of children playing in the park,
                              dancing and screaming.
It tastes like a comfortable chocolate cake bed.
Its smell is like a hint of fudge cooking from the local bakery.
Laughter looks like the sight of an upside down frown.
Laughter feels like your heart beating with joy.
It reminds me of a hot summer's day.

Adam Palfrey (9)
Christ Church Primary School, Weston-super-Mare

Silence

Silence is golden, like a fish in the sea.
It sounds like the wind in the night sky.
It tastes like white chocolate which most people love.
It smells like food in an oven.
It looks like a diamond that glistens in the night when it's dark.
It feels soft and silky.
It reminds people of stars.

Harry Miller (10)
Christ Church Primary School, Weston-super-Mare

Love

Love is red like a Valentine's card that is like the fire.
It sounds like a heart that is beating for a long time.
It tastes like a melting chocolate that dribbles down your mouth.
It smells like perfume that sprays around the whole room.
It looks like a heart that is pumping blood.
It feels like foam when you put your feet into it.
It reminds me of a strawberry just ripened.

Oliver Marston (9)
Christ Church Primary School, Weston-super-Mare

Fear

Fear tastes like hot burning lava, that scorches your mouth.
It's red and black with danger.
You can't see it but it's always there.
It's as high as Heaven and as wide as a football pitch.
It smells like a bonfire burning hot.
It feels like rough wood and it reminds me of vampires.
It sounds like a howling werewolf in the mist.

Ewan Tyler-Schofield (9)
Christ Church Primary School, Weston-super-Mare

Anger

Anger is like a hot red sun showering angry rays on the world.
It tastes like the taste of sour chilli that stings your tongue.
It sounds like thunder and lions roaring.
It feels like burning lava, so hot that it turns metal white.
It looks like people having waves of anger and strength
                                                    coming from them.
It feels like red, red fire all around you.

Anna Carvanova (9)
Christ Church Primary School, Weston-super-Mare

Sadness

Sadness is light grey like when a fire goes out.
It tastes like water, plain and odd.
It looks like a gloomy fog that's in your path and
                              you can't get through.
It sounds like silence and too quiet.
It smells like smoke from a fireplace that's just been put out.
It feels like nobody's there and you're all on your own
                              in a dark room.
It reminds me of a sad day.

Jake Griffin (9)
Christ Church Primary School, Weston-super-Mare

Happiness

Happiness is yellow like sunflowers
and stars in the sky shining so bright.
It sounds like people having a good time.
It tastes like ice cream.
It smells like buttercups.
It looks like the best day ever.
It feels like a cuddly bear.
It reminds me of the sun.

Megan Baker (9)
Christ Church Primary School, Weston-super-Mare

Happiness

Happiness is light blue like the shining sky.
It sounds like angels whistling with joy.
It tastes like light chocolate in the sun.
It smells like clouds floating around.
It looks like fresh air blowing by.
It feels like light blue tears of happiness.
It reminds me of summer holidays
and angels singing and flying around.

Harry King (9)
Christ Church Primary School, Weston-super-Mare

Happiness

Happiness is a nice little sunshine in the sky.
Birds flying all around you.
It tastes like a banana, all smooth and creamy.
It's a cool glass of water when you're really hot.
It smells like sunflowers, brilliant and tall.
It's fluffy, sticky candyfloss and a woolly sheep's coat
                                keeping me warm and cosy.
It looks like a field of shiny green grass.
A day at the beach when the sand is soft and I build tall
Sandcastles and listen to the seagulls squawking and screeching.

Chantelle Jackson-Poole (9)
Christ Church Primary School, Weston-super-Mare

Fear

Fear is red, like your heart beating fast.
It sounds like thunder roaring outside, trapping you in,
waking my heart with fear and dread.
It tastes like cold blood running through your heart.
It smells like smoke from a fire as you walk out of the house.
It looks like a ball of danger coming towards us, orange and red.
It feels like the cold rain on your head.
It reminds me of flames flying up and up.

Layla Essamadi (9)
Christ Church Primary School, Weston-super-Mare

Silence

Silence is blank like white.
It tastes like vanilla ice cream.
It smells like a playground heating up in the sun.
It looks like a weird house.
It feels like an empty cold room.
It reminds me of outer space
where there is no sound or movement.

Alex Raymond (9)
Christ Church Primary School, Weston-super-Mare

Silence

What is silence?
Is it when you cannot hear a thing
And you feel isolated and alone?
Is it blue like waves rolling into the sand?
Is it on the moor when you only hear rivers and birds?

What is silence?
Is it when you hear babies crying,
Tears streaming down their faces?
Is it the wind on a cold misty morning
Or is it the sun shining on the sea?

What is silence?
In some cases it is terrifying.
In others it is as sweet and lovely as a rose.
Silence is the waves, the wind and the sun.
Silence is the birds, the rivers and tears.
Silence can be hearing everything
And hearing nothing.

Amy Reade (10)
Colston's Girls' School, Bristol

Who Am I?

Her furry coat is brown and white,
She sleeps all day and plays all night.
Her tiny pink nose is rather cute,
Twitching and sniffing as she plays in her chute.
Nibbling on treats and storing them away,
Go back and find them another day.
Can you guess who she is yet?
You may not have met,
The prettiest pet by far,
Harriet the hamster . . . what a superstar!

Libby Morris (11)
Colston's Girls' School, Bristol

Hate

It is black,
Like a black snake coming to attack,
like a killer waiting to kill.
It smells like chilli powder
in a hot steamy mouth,
burning its way to the end.
It looks like stabbing Death's black heart
and blood coming out.
It looks like a killer has made his move.
It looks like stars
falling out of the sky.
It feels like death is coming your way.
It feels like a bomb has hit your friends.
It feels like you're the only one left.
It feels like you're not there.
It reminds me of life coming to an end.
It reminds me of nothing in the air.
It reminds me of someone taking out my heart.
It reminds me of God with two heads, both bad.
It tastes like steam
steaming through you.
It sounds like spiders moving around you.
It sounds like . . . *me.*

Flora Hodges (10)
Colston's Girls' School, Bristol

Silence

Silence is grey.
It sounds like an empty classroom
When someone calls.
It feels like you're in a cold dark night.
It tastes like stale air.
It's like you're on your own.
Silence reminds me of losing my mum.
It smells cold and damp.

Isobel Reid (10)
Colston's Girls' School, Bristol

Fire

I can taste sick
and blood and fear,
thrown in with dry sand.

There are screeching yells in my ears,
echoing all around.
I can hear pumps of my heart,
getting faster by the second.

I can see fire,
flaming, scorching, flaring,
reaching way up to the sky.
Everything's getting faster and faster
more blurred than ever.

I'm sick, scared, terrified, horrified.
Just one more could cause me to die.

My fear is orange,
like sad, angry churning inside my body.
Closing around me.

It feels like spiders
and bats in my stomach.
I'm sweating like mad
but frozen still.

My mouth has turned to stone
and my eyes are glued open.
I hate the feeling
and never want to feel it again.

Charlotte Crooke (10)
Colston's Girls' School, Bristol

Magic Spell

I wave my magic wand,
To cast a spell of mine.
I could cast a spell on you
And you shrink right down your spine.

My spell looks like a monster
A deer about to prance.
It looks like a rock 'n' roll pig
Who you know is about to dance.

It smells like a deodorant,
It sticks to everything.
It smells of something bad
And it gives a nasty sting.

It tastes like a hot egg
And you know that hurts a lot.
It tastes like some boiling food,
Bubbling in a great big pot.

It reminds me of a place
Where everything looks the same.
It reminds me of a dog,
He's trained and very tame.

Now, I drink the spell myself.
It runs up and down my knee,
But although I feel crazy,
It is all just magical me.

Susanna Lee (10)
Colston's Girls' School, Bristol

Sadness

A dull grey hidden away from the rest of the world.
The face of a weeping angel hiding in the darkness.
The burn of tears flooding down a pale face,
cheeks red with anger.
The day my grandpa died, the tears and frowns,
the karma had been spoiled.
Sadness smells of salty tears,
sour like soap in your mouth, throbbing in pain.
It tastes like a bitter lemon,
the sticky juice running down your chin
leaving a mark forever.

Imogen Cox (11)
Colston's Girls' School, Bristol

Fear Poem

It smells like a burnt out candle
that never relights
it's all black
and I start spinning
faster and faster, quicker and quicker
it's all dizzy!
I don't know what is happening!
It feels like the sun
never burning out
but coming closer and closer.
My heart gets faster
as I run away from it.
I can see the light fading away
like a black cloud moving on.
It tastes like the tears of children
and the sound of a beating heart
never stopping!

Emma Holt (10)
Colston's Girls' School, Bristol

Sadness

It is grey and weary like a morning fog,
You feel alone like you're on a life-long jog.

If I could touch it I would push it away,
Never to come back and never ruin my day.

Sadness is an emotion, a deadly potion,
Which is hard to help or ignore.
When you feel sad, all around you is bad,
Your eyes are all puffy and sore.

Sadness feels like an illness, like a horrible bug,
It can hang around for ages but is helped by a hug.

Catherine Gould (11)
Colston's Girls' School, Bristol

Fear And Darkness

The colour of darkness is the colour of fear,
I'm stuck in the darkness, and he's still here.
I smell his dark side in the darkness
And it looks like he has a harness.
I feel his torch burning my skin,
So I must get rid of him.
I taste the dirt from when I fell over
And I have ruined my new pullover.
I look at his big bulldog,
Compared to that, I'm a bullfrog.
The sound of his voice,
Is such a noise.
He's shouting and bawling
And I'm now falling.
But I know I will always lose.

Elizabeth Williams (10)
Colston's Girls' School, Bristol

My Secret Love

It's dinnertime,
with my father, brothers and sisters.
He comes - my love
and waves through the window.
I sneak off out of the room
and there he is,
waiting for me under a tree.
He is sat on the bench gleaming.
We dance and sing,
and sing and dance.
And while we are dancing,
very quickly,
no longer than a second,
he kisses me
and runs away with glee.
I scream joyfully in the rain,
and spin around.
I climb my vine,
up to my bedroom,
and there is my father,
waiting for me . . .

Yasmin Davis (10)
Colston's Girls' School, Bristol

Some People Say . . .

Some people say my mum is a fool,
how can she be when she's got a pool.

Some people say my dad is bad
but he's really not, he's mad!

Some people say my sister is cool,
I don't think she is, she makes me drool!

Some people say my cat's fat,
she could fall down, *splat!*

Daisy Cullen (10)
Colston's Girls' School, Bristol

I Fear . . .

I fear my stepdad:
He is hunting me down,
There he is in the distance,
I need to escape.

I fear his hands,
As they hit me and slap me,
He is rough,
I am weak.

I fear his gun,
As he tries to shoot me,
It is powerful,
Knocking me down.

I fear his face,
As he screams and shouts,
It turns red with fury,
If I do wrong.

It feels like wolves are after me,
Ready to kill,
He has high standards,
Out of my reach.

I fear most things,
But my stepdad the most.

Ellie Lawrence (10)
Colston's Girls' School, Bristol

Evil

It's red and black,
like a spider waiting to catch you.

It has many forms, all equally as evil as the next.
Fear, death, abuse, hate.

If you touch it your hand recoils
and your heart stops beating.

It sounds like an infinite echo,
never stopping and wherever you are it's still there.

It tastes disgusting and overwhelming,
so you would quickly spit it out.

Phoebe Thompson (10)
Colston's Girls' School, Bristol

The Sand

I'm the sand,
I'm like a yellow blanket,
Covering and following parts of the sea.
Sometimes the sea grasps at my precious treasures.
I think the sea is mean and ghastly
Stealing away the gifts that he has given me.
I hear the sea roaring into my face.
I feel people's feet tramping over me
And spades digging and shovelling through me.
If I hear the children laugh and throw me about
I feel glad that I'm helping them have fun
And the nasty sea takes the children's treasures.
But at the end of the day
Strokes me gently
And it is time to sleep, sleep, sleep.

Naomi Gibson (8)
Deerhurst & Apperley CE Primary School, Gloucester

The Sea

The sea is like a roaring bear,
It waves, it roars, it tears
It grumbles in the dawn
It waves in the morn
It tears at the rocks
It mothers to the sea life
The seagulls call their call
In the early dawn.

The sea is like a roaring bear,
The night skies calm it down
It swifts, it swoops
It loops the loop
It starts to grumble
When it sees the sky
Turning yellow with the glow of the golden sun
It starts to get rough again.

Sarah Parker (10)
Deerhurst & Apperley CE Primary School, Gloucester

Socks

Big socks, small socks, long socks and short socks.
Small socks and clean socks.
Red, blue, pink, purple and stripy socks.
Smelly socks and holes in the toe socks.
Cartoon socks, sensible socks
But warm socks.

Storm Barlow (7)
Deerhurst & Apperley CE Primary School, Gloucester

The Magic Box

(Based on 'Magic Box' by Kit Wright)

I will put in the box . . .
The swish of the salty sea
The fire out of the nose of a Chinese dragon
The music from a violin.

I will put in the box . . .
The notes trying to squeeze out of a recorder
The piano thumping as the people play it
The scrape of a bow playing the violin.

I will put in the box . . .
The loudness of a cello playing
The smell of perfumed flowers
The crackle and crunch of fallen leaves.

I will put in the box . . .
The breeze of the wind blowing through the air
The confidence of reading a book
The heat of a fiery sun and the gentle light of the moon.

My box is made from the sparkle of the stars.

Ellie Pitt (8)
Deerhurst & Apperley CE Primary School, Gloucester

My Dog

I love my dog, he is the best.
He is the best amongst the rest.

He goes for walks all the time,
Whether it's snowy, rainy or fine.

He eats his tea greedily.
He asks for more by raising a paw.

He sleeps all night and plays all day.
I miss my dog when I'm away.

Isabel Beckett (7)
Deerhurst & Apperley CE Primary School, Gloucester

The Magic Box

(Based on 'Magic Box' by Kit Wright)

I will put in the box . . .
The taste of a red apple when you bite into it.
A tough tooth from a big beaver.
The hot sun from the soft clouds.

I will put in the box . . .
The blue water from the Pacific Ocean.
The eyeball from a great white shark.
The smell of ashes from a burning bonfire.

I will put in the box . . .
The palm trees from Australian beaches.
The firefly from a German rainforest.
The noise of a loud buggy.

My box is made of . . .
Gold and silver crystals
And hinges made of volcanic rock.

Scott Trower (7)
Deerhurst & Apperley CE Primary School, Gloucester

Collecting Conkers

Looking for conkers on the ground.
Looking for conkers round and brown.
Kicking up leaves red and green.
Picking up conkers that I have seen.
Collecting conkers hard and shiny.
Collecting conkers big and tiny.
Looking for conkers here and there.
Looking for conkers everywhere.

Hollie Ennis (7)
Deerhurst & Apperley CE Primary School, Gloucester

The Magic Box

(Based on 'Magic Box' by Kit Wright)

I will put in the box . . .

A dapple grey horse with a snowy white mane and tail.
A glossy chocolatey brown saddle.
A pure black head collar with reins.

I will put in the box . . .

The taste of smooth Galaxy chocolate.
The smell of salt being sprinkled onto cod in batter and chips.
The sound of small animals playing happily together.
The touch of a dolphin's smooth skin.

My box is fashioned from wood from the oldest oak tree.
Sparkling jewels decorate it.
The jewels are emeralds, sapphires, topaz, amethysts,
Clear diamonds and smooth, white, shiny pearls.

Abigail Platt (7)
Deerhurst & Apperley CE Primary School, Gloucester

The Sea

The sea is like a raging bull
Lashing against the sandy rocks,
Endlessly it searches for its prey
Then strikes against the sandy beach,
Covering the rock pools that stick out beneath.
The sea roars!
Its prey will run but can never hide!
Because then the sea covers most land,
It roars and roars!
Then at night you can hear screams of death
In its sandy cave . . .
When divers dive in the cave!
They see bones . . . bones . . . and more
Bones!

Ben Adams (10)
Deerhurst & Apperley CE Primary School, Gloucester

The Sea

I am the sea

I am like a raging horse
Bashing against the sandy beach

I am like an elephant
Spurting water out of my trunk

People swim on me, having fun
I would like a friend

I can push boats around
So be warned!

Keep on sailing and playing
I won't harm you

I am the biggest
So I am the boss

You can't kill me luckily!

Morgan Stancer (8)
Deerhurst & Apperley CE Primary School, Gloucester

The Sea

The sea is like a powerful horse
Galloping towards the beach and back again
Changing colours as it comes.
All the colours of the sea
The sea is like a butterfly
Spreading out its wings.
The sea is like a tie-dye blanket
Waving up and down.
I go past the golden sand every day.
The colours of the kelp
Changing colour
Wiggling around inside me.

Kitty Roberts (9)
Deerhurst & Apperley CE Primary School, Gloucester

The Sea

The sea is like an elephant spurting water out of its trunk.
As the elephant spurts, it stomps and causes waves to rage.
As the elephant swings its trunk whirlpool's form.

As the elephant splashes, the tide comes in.
As the elephant strolls around it crushes rocks
And turns them into stones,
Some form into sand on the tide, others don't.
The elephant takes revenge on humankind
So it creates whirlpools, waves and a storm,
Even the tide comes in, it is so angry.
When it wants food it uses its trunk and catches some fish.
Nobody or nothing gets past the Oceanphant alive.

Joe Nicholas (8)
Deerhurst & Apperley CE Primary School, Gloucester

The Sea's Aspects

The sea is like a collapsing chasm
Curling into oblivion
Things get sucked down.
You can hear their screams
Even the sharks are scared of them,
But only as the night draws near,
In the morning when the sun is high in the sky
The sea is like a playful puppy
Using the divers as a ball.
It only wants to play and have some fun.
Being nice and being bad
Are only a couple of its aspects,
It likes the divers and surfers
And the things deep down in its watery heart.

Sam Topham (9)
Deerhurst & Apperley CE Primary School, Gloucester

The Sea Dog

I am the Sea Dog.
In the morning
I hit the stupid little rocks.
At night I eat the sand and spit it out.
The earth infuriates me sometimes
And I gobble up the cities with my mouth open wide.
The rocks dream of being bigger than me but they never will be.
My giant empire is guarded by my soldiers,
My loyal guards for my life.
The clouds are my slaves, they keep me big and strong.
Nothing will beat me.
When the ice melts I will be free.

Andrew Torr (9)
Deerhurst & Apperley CE Primary School, Gloucester

The Sea

The sea is like a raging wild whip,
Lashing out at the rocks and sand.
Lashing, lashing.
Endlessly taking back its children of the sand,
Feeding on them. They are never to be seen again.
Sometimes on stormy nights you can hear their screams.
And if you are lucky you can see the ghostly horseman.
Seeking his revenge, slashing away at anything in his path.
How could you stop him?
No one knows, but maybe you hold the secret
We will never know.

Scott Gibson (10)
Deerhurst & Apperley CE Primary School, Gloucester

The Sand

I am the sand.
I hate it when people walk all over me.
It is painful because sometimes shoes kick me around.
The grey and blue sea crashes against me from the air.
Deckchairs dig their way into my skin.
The sea is much, much bigger than me on the beach.
Sometimes sand buggies drive over me and it is painful.
The sand is a fudge colour.
I am afraid I might get washed away.

Matthew Benson (8)
Deerhurst & Apperley CE Primary School, Gloucester

The Sea

The rain crashes down on the sea like an eagle
And as the rain hits the growling water big splashes appear,
Soon after the storm it gets soft,
Under the sea, sharks whoosh their tails
And eat their prey,
Turtles slowly go past as a sea wreck slowly sinks,
A squealing squid calls to its partner
As a seasnake covers itself in sand
And scares the flat fish away.

Harry Stephens (8)
Deerhurst & Apperley CE Primary School, Gloucester

The Sea

The sea is like an angry dog
Biting at the rock.
It chews away at the chalky white cliffs
With sharp grey teeth.
It is like a giant dog.

Jonathon Askey (8)
Deerhurst & Apperley CE Primary School, Gloucester

Treasure Chest

I love seasalt, it keeps me healthy,
Although the sea to me is like a bully.

I cough and I splutter from the sea,
Just like the sea wants me, wants me for tea.

When divers come I keep dead still,
I really don't want to be cooked on a grill!

I am wishing, longing for a friend,
So please come and join me before the end.

Julia Parsonage (8)
Deerhurst & Apperley CE Primary School, Gloucester

The Rock

I am a rock,
The big bullying sea likes to push me around,
I am tired of it,
I would like to be bigger than the blue bully
But at least it covers me up like a duvet in the night,
But when morning comes it acts like a raging dog,
Nudging people off bodyboards.
I see the boards wink at me.

Ben Green (9)
Deerhurst & Apperley CE Primary School, Gloucester

The Sea

The sea is like a lion
Pouncing on its prey
Then dragging it back into its cave
And going back out for more
And as it gets more food it starts to get fuller and fuller
Calmer and calmer, then it goes calm
And doesn't go out anymore.

Jessica Beckett (8)
Deerhurst & Apperley CE Primary School, Gloucester

The Sea

I am the whinnying horse of the sea,
And this is what I want to be.
I bring life,
Cut sand like a knife,
I am free -
I am the sea!

I am the whinnying horse of the sea,
And this is what I want to be.
I am strong,
I work all day long,
I am free -
I am the sea!

I am the whinnying horse of the sea,
And this is what I want to be.
I go in and out,
I move about,
I am free -
I am the sea!

I am the whinnying horse of the sea,
And this is what I want to be.
I thrash the rocks
And fishermen's stocks,
I am free -
I am the sea!

I am the whinnying horse of the sea,
And this is what I want to be.
I devour the sand,
I eat the land,
I am free -
I am the sea!

Esther Street (9)
Deerhurst & Apperley CE Primary School, Gloucester

The Sand

The sea is like a bull raging towards me,
It tries to take me away
As it chews away at me bit by bit.

I remember centuries ago when I was a rock,
I stay buried so I'm safe from the sea taking me away.

The sea rolls on the beach all day.
Crushing rocks into pebbles and stones.

The sea is like a wolf grabbing on its prey,
I am its prey.

Henry O'Niell (8)
Deerhurst & Apperley CE Primary School, Gloucester

The Fish

The fish are like clouds in the sky,
Moving in the wind.
They get carried around from place to place
Moving away from home.
Fish cry with the coldness of the bullying sea.
Stranded, lonely, bored,
Bored with swimming through shipwrecks,
Bored with being cased by sharks,
Bored with divers catching them.
The fish are tiny rainbows,
Full of colours,
Full of shimmers,
Full of life.

Maddi O'Niell (10)
Deerhurst & Apperley CE Primary School, Gloucester

The Sand

The sand buries our feet.
The sand is squishy when you get too close to the sea.
The sand squiggles up together.
You can make a sandcastle.
You can make a sand bell.
The sand is flat.
The sand is soggy.
The sand is soft.
The sand comes in different colours.

Olivia Pike (9)
Deerhurst & Apperley CE Primary School, Gloucester

Guess My Love

I have a pet, she's gold and white.
Cute at night,
She looks at me,
She's helpful, always protective,
She will always be treated by me.

Her name is Aby.
She's a white banded cinnamon hamster
And she lets me feed her and play.
Away she runs, every day.
I feed her radishes for a treat,
But it never stops her going to sleep.

Isaac Whitehead (7)
Easton Royal Primary School, Pewsey

The Football Match

The ball was passed back
And my teammate gave it a thwack!
I nodded it on with my head
And passed it on to Fred,
Fred went for the slide
And kicked the ball out wide,
The referee gave out a red
I'm sorry it went to Fred
As I'm dribbling down the wing
I can hear the crowd starting to sing
I use a bit of control
Then I shoot and score a goal!

Billy Rudolph (9)
Easton Royal Primary School, Pewsey

F1 Racing

The green flag falling,
The stench of fuel filling the air.
Engines as loud as thunder,
The wind racing past me,
As I speed down the road,
The cars slipping backwards
And then I crash into a wall.
Wheels flying in the air,
Engine on fire,
Jumping out of my car just in time,
As I see all the cars at the finish line.

Ted Yeates (10)
Easton Royal Primary School, Pewsey

That's My Dog, Saki

Black and hairy,
Not at all scary!
Playful and fun,
Gets hot in the sun.
Eats apples and berries,
Tomatoes and cherries!
Loves to chase a rabbit,
His only bad habit.
He's sleek and thin,
Has spots on his chin.
He wees in puddles
And loves his cuddles.
He swims in the canal,
Which he does very well.
I tell him to sit,
He does quite a bit.
He runs so fast,
I can never get past.
He's soft to touch,
I love him so much.

Not at all barky,
That's my dog, Saki.

Simone Hamblin (8)
Easton Royal Primary School, Pewsey

School

We go to school
And play in the pool

The harder we work
The better the perk.

We do have play,
But sometimes stay.

School is great,
So we mustn't be late.

Molly Grant (8)
Easton Royal Primary School, Pewsey

Railway

R ailways are one of my hobbies
A rail is made of steel
I like all railways, but especially EWS and MHR,
L iking railways is a good thing to like,
W atercress Line is another name for the company MHR,
A cton in London is a depot for the company EWS,
Y ou and I can have fun riding on railways!

Josh Macbeth (9)
Easton Royal Primary School, Pewsey

My Pet Finn

My pet is called Finn
And she likes to swim

She goes in the sea
And shakes water at me

The kids throw her balls
And she comes when she's called

She likes to lick lollies
But she's a diabetic doggy!

Olivia Dufour (7)
Easton Royal Primary School, Pewsey

Sparkle

Sparkle's my cuddly toy
Sparkles just like the sky
But she never hides
Pink and fluffy
Soft as a bunny
She's there for me at night.

Ellie Powell (7)
Easton Royal Primary School, Pewsey

My Dog Patch

I've got a dog called Patch,
who'll try to snatch,
any edible item
from anywhere,
if it's new or old.

I've got a Dalmatian called Patch
who'll try, but can't catch
his favourite toy 'Mankie',
but after that he'll go and chew
my dad's old snotty hankie!

Jack Harvey (10)
Easton Royal Primary School, Pewsey

Save Them!

Wolves are sweet and cuddly
but people think they're mean.

Wolves are endangered,
we're killing them, us, you, me.

I love them and want one as a pet,
through the forest they run.

Save them!

Sophie Butcher (9)
Hillesley CE VA Primary School, Hillesley

Dog Fun!

D ogs are really good fun.
O ver the fields they love to run.
G rowl at people nobody know,
S o I wonder what it's like
    to be a dog chasing birds, maybe crows!

Faye Young (9)
Hillesley CE VA Primary School, Hillesley

Animals

A n animal is an amazing creature,
N ever get it wrong,
I love animals all round the world,
M aybe even in Hong Kong,
A n animal can be thin or wide,
L ots are short and long,
S ometimes animals can be scary
    but they are the best thing in the *world!*

Charlotte Rowberry (10)
Hillesley CE VA Primary School, Hillesley

Tiger

T hrough the long grass, you can see his eyes.
I n the jungle he's the king.
G ross poachers love the skin.
E xcited people look for them.
R un tiger run.

Joseph Moore (9)
Hillesley CE VA Primary School, Hillesley

Street Racing

F ast and
A mazingly ballistic
S tripes and
T ries to pose and

C ommit a crime,
A t sunset they're in the street.
R acing until
S undown when they flee.

Fintan Holder (10)
Hillesley CE VA Primary School, Hillesley

Endangered Animals

E nglish people hunt for animals,
N ever caring what they destroy,
D angerous darts speed through the air,
A nimals are the best,
N ever ever kill them,
G orillas and
E lephants and
R hinos need protection.

Emily Hayward (10)
Hillesley CE VA Primary School, Hillesley

A Childhood Memory

When I swam with dolphins, it was very fun
Splashing about inside the pool under the Mexican sun

Dolphins coming up to me so I could hold their fin
And as they passed in front of me, I felt their soft, soft skin

Jumping in the air over the water right up high
I thought they were going to disappear into the sky

They touched the water softly as they began to fall
They dived into the blue and hardly made a splash at all

The dolphins swam right by me as if to say hello
I felt their gentle nature and just didn't want to go.

I will not forget the kindness that the dolphins gave to me
They were as cute and cuddly as my teddy.

Rhion Butcher (9)
Hillesley CE VA Primary School, Hillesley

The Elephant

Elephant, elephant, stamping around
on the ground or in the mud.

Elephant, elephant big and tall
rolling around in the mud.
Enormous ears, giant feet and a marvellous tail.
Nice and strong for defence.
Nice shining white tusks for elephant.

Elephant, elephant, big and strong
with beautiful colours for decoration.

Elephant, elephant, stamping with his feet
and the sound he makes with his mouth.

Yazmine MacQuarrie (10)
Holway Park Primary School, Taunton

The Elephant

What a great creature with beautiful shiny tusks,
What amazing gigantic ears swishing about,
Giant legs like tree trunks,
Trunk like a slithering snake.

Watch it roll in the mud, how fantastic,
There it goes with its herd,
Look at the trunk swish freely,
What beautiful painted patterns on the body.

Enormous elephant, so peaceful and proud,
Stomp, stomp, stomp,
The elephant is stomping over peacefully,
Tall like a house,
But elephants never forget.

Katy Greatrex (10)
Holway Park Primary School, Taunton

The Magnificent Creature

Indian elephant with gigantic feet,
giant tusks that are white and shiny,
enormous trunk that is extraordinary,
magnificent painted patterns that stand out bold.
This is a magnificent creature
with an enormous body.
Heavy and gigantic yet really peaceful,
it has amazing ears so it can hear.

Sasha Carp (10)
Holway Park Primary School, Taunton

Elephants

Elephant, elephant,
Big and bright
Dull and grey,
He's rough like rocks
And tough like a wall.

Giant feet,
Amazing ears
The swaying trunk
And shiny tusks.

Dean Lepage (10)
Holway Park Primary School, Taunton

Harvest

H arvest is here again
A nd I smell veg
R ain falls
V eg grows
E very time
S ummer is here
T he rain falls.

Curtis Clark (9)
Holway Park Primary School, Taunton

Indian Elephant

Indian elephant, dark as mud,
By the river of the earth,
What small tail, what great feet,
Loving the mud of thy God.

Here comes the festival of light,
With the elephants dressed up bright,
Pretty patterns, beautiful white tusks,
Loving the mud as thy God.

Eyes as big as tennis balls,
Ears as big as tennis rackets,
Trunk as long as a telephone pole,
Loving the mud of thy God.

Michael Stanford (10)
Holway Park Primary School, Taunton

Harvest

H arvest apples, so juicy
A pples are green and red
R eady to eat
V ery delicious
E at it fast
S uper tasty
T astes great.

Matthew Trump (9)
Holway Park Primary School, Taunton

Apples

I love apples so much
But not as much as the harvest.
I want to grow an apple
But my mum does not.
I love apples.

Alice Staple (8)
Holway Park Primary School, Taunton

Old Dogs

Eyes like puddles of blue
Ears like a fluffy bow
Mouths so big they could eat a car
And they smell worse than skunks
Bed so comfy like beanbags
Plus it says lazy all over their nametags
All they do is eat all day
So all we do is pay pay pay!
This is what an old dog is *hip hip hooray!*

Jordon Bolwell (10)
Ivy Lane Primary School, Chippenham

The Weather

I am the sun
as yellow as can be.

I am the wind
as relaxed as can be.

I am the rain
as hard as can be.

I am the snow
as fun as can be.

I am the ice
as dangerous as can be.

I am the fog
as thick as can be.

I am the weather
Do you like me?

Ayla Exton (10)
Ivy Lane Primary School, Chippenham

The Horror House

In the gloomy house
lived a vicious mouse.
He liked his home
even though he lived in a dome.

One morning a kid stepped on the lawn
out came a monster with a horn.
The kids ran so fast
the monster lost track of the past.

The next day the kid said the house is crazy
so the monster came out all hazy.
The kid stayed this time
whilst the monster did a crime . . .

Daniel Griggs (11)
Ivy Lane Primary School, Chippenham

Football

Goal scorer
Striker
Good footballer
Fast runner
Cup winner
Good shooter
Great header
Brilliant tackler
High jumper
Great passer
Amazing penalty taker
Goalkeeper
Winner!

Joe Hewitt-Long (11)
Ivy Lane Primary School, Chippenham

Racing!

Today is the day of the race
I am going to win
I feel like a cheetah raring to go
Bang!
There I go, full of energy -
5th place going on 4th
Heart pumping so fast
My hair all fuzzy
I want to win!
The wind blowing in my face
Gasping for air and breath
Need to speed up a bit
Getting closer to the finish line
I am . . .
        The winner!

Chloë Cunningham (10)
Ivy Lane Primary School, Chippenham

Boats

Sun seekers are speeding across the sea
Making lots of waves
Where are they going?
The beach to have fun
Are they going on an adventure
To distant lands afar?
Going to get some treasure to put
In a jar

Sun seekers' boats are cool!

Matthew Barrington (10)
Ivy Lane Primary School, Chippenham

The Sweet Shop

Can you see the sweets,
Stacked in the window now,
I'm getting hungry now,
Groan, moan, groan!

Race you to the shop,
Oh no! I'm out of money now,
Can you please! Lend me some now,
Groan, moan, groan!

Look at the chocolate,
Getting bought right now.
Oh, I wish I was them now,
Groan, moan groan!

Look at that girl,
Eating a toffee apple now.
Wait, she's getting fat now!
Oh no! Oh no! Oh no!

Poppy Selman (10)
Ivy Lane Primary School, Chippenham

Football

Goal scorer
Super striker
Amazing defence
Players in formation
Running for a goal
Gerrard takes a penalty
He scores
        A goal!

Adam Frampton (10)
Ivy Lane Primary School, Chippenham

Jumping Jazzie's Restaurant

At jumping Jazzie's restaurant
The gateaux is gritty,
The beans black,
Slugs stuffed in the sponge,
What do you think about that?

There are mouldy maggots in the moussaka,
The curry full of old cod,
The toffee tasteless
And hard peas with the pasta.
What do you think about that?

I don't know why they're complaining
Because the food I cook is nice,
I am the next Gordon Ramsey
There's no denying that.

Now I am really rich
And very soon to be,
The world's next famous chef,
Presenting 'The F Word' on TV.

Jasmin Barber (11)
Ivy Lane Primary School, Chippenham

The Monster In My Bed!

The monster in my bed is green.
He is always in my bed.
I always call my mum
But she never hears me.
I'm in the attic now -
He's got eyes of flame
And never goes away.
I hate monsters now so go away - please!

Sophie Hanks (10)
Ivy Lane Primary School, Chippenham

Guess What?

I am brown all over,
People love to eat me,
I can be crunchy and munchy or hard and solid,
You can find me in a sweet shop,
My wrappers can be colourful,
What am I?
I am a flavour of an ice cream,
I can be shaped all different sizes,
I am out of this galaxy,
I've been to Mars and back,
I've seen the Milky Way,
Resist me if you can,
What am I?

Amy Dolman (10)
Ivy Lane Primary School, Chippenham

What Am I?

I pop
I bash
I fall in the trash!
I grow
I flow
I'm like a bow and arrow
And I fly like a sparrow
I sparkle
I flash
And form a big crash!
I distracted the lorry
Which fell in the quarry!
I dash
I mash
I cost a lot of cash!
Finally I make a great big clash!

I am a . . . ?

Edward Sawyer (10)
Ivy Lane Primary School, Chippenham

The Planet

T he planet is blue, yellow, red and green
H ave you seen our crops of happy beans?
E agles, lions, tigers and more

P eople watch volcanoes, erupting from the core
L et yourself go on the planet
A nyone can get wet
N o one is bad on this happy place
E veryone together whatever their race
T ime to go, sad to see you leave.

Alice Richards (11)
Ivy Lane Primary School, Chippenham

Fireworks

I bang
I grow
I sizzle
and flow

I pop
I bash
I fly
and crash

I swirl
I twirl
I sparkle
and whirl

I dash
I mash
I light
and flash

I fizz
I whizz
I burst
at first.

Kane Fernandez (10)
Ivy Lane Primary School, Chippenham

The Beach

Can we go to the beach now?
Look at the coach now,
Come on, get your shoes on,
Wow! Wow! Wow!

Where is the train now?
I am getting bored now,
Can I have a drink now?
Wow! Wow! Wow!

Look at the beach now,
When is the train stopping now?
Where can we sit now?
Wow! Wow! Wow!

Can we go in the sea now?
Why aren't the floats blown up now?
I want an ice cream now!
Wow! Wow! Wow!

The sea is cold now,
Can we go home now?
I am wet now,
Wow! Wow! Wow!

Katherine Sawyer (10)
Ivy Lane Primary School, Chippenham

Fox

Chicken nicker
Garbage picker
Farmer's anger
Garden hanger
Poor breeder
Meat needer
Night spyer
Trouble trier.

Jesse Gibbs (11)
Ivy Lane Primary School, Chippenham

The Disastrous House Party

There was once a girl, spoilt rotten,
How much she owned, she had forgotten,
She felt so lucky,
Without getting mucky,
She bought a brand, a brand new dress made of cotton.

And with this beautiful cotton dress,
Without making an entire mess,
She invited her school,
To a party quite cool,
But was a lady in distress.

The school arrived at seven
And were there 'til eleven,
The house was a mess
And as for the dress,
The girl felt like going to Heaven.

The girl's father who was quite plain,
Had a beard like a lion's mane,
Came back to the mess,
He got into a stress
And the girl was never seen again!

Charlotte Brown (10)
Ivy Lane Primary School, Chippenham

Snowflake

It's Tuesday morning, it's snowing,
My school has been closed for a day!
I see a snowflake on the window,
Now I've got to get dressed, I've told my snowflake to stay.
But forgot all about it, when I went out to play,
I got back just after teatime to check on my snowflake,
But sadly it was gone!

Krystina Clark (10)
Ivy Lane Primary School, Chippenham

My Hamster

Running round and round her cage,
Maybe she will be on stage,
Zooming to her food quite fast,
Hopefully she won't need a cast.

Scurries round her cage at night,
Sometimes she will give a fright!

She is so cuddly and soft,
Once we found her in the loft,
Up the bars she will climb,
But she will always take her time.

She is such a sweetheart.
Ouch! She bit me!
Watch out.

Charlotte Sawyer (10)
Ivy Lane Primary School, Chippenham

Killer Animals

Killed by the cats
And slobbered by the dog!
Harassed by hamsters
And battered by the hog!

Strangled by the snakes
And scratched by the bears!
Poisoned by the skunk
And teased by the hares!

Laughed at by the monkeys,
Bullied by the baboon!
Flattened by the elephant
And thumped by the racoon!

Georgina Dalton (10)
Ivy Lane Primary School, Chippenham

Friends

Friends will fight,
Friends will play,
Sometimes friends split up, leaving you upset
Or maybe leave you out,
It can sometimes leave you feeling sick.

Friends will let you down, leaving you worried,
Sometimes friends can be fun to be with.
You can have pillow fights at sleepovers.
You could watch movies all night,
Or maybe even get in trouble and stay awake all night
And drive your parents up the wall,
But best of all, friends are for life.

Jessica Fuller (10)
Ivy Lane Primary School, Chippenham

Dragons

Fire breather,
Six limbs,
Fire breather,
Four legs, two wings.
Fire breather,
Fire, fire flyer!

Livestock raider,
Knight fire fighter,
I wonder if one still lives?
Knight fighter,
Livestock raider,
Is that what Nessie really is?
I'm at Loch Ness,
On the good ship Bess,
And what's that floating in the water?
It's a dragon!

Arren Roach (10)
Ivy Lane Primary School, Chippenham

My Sister

My sister is the queen of devil land,
She is the leader of the bad band!
Her nickname is terror child,
And she is not mild!

Doctor Who is her idol,
And sometimes I feel suicidal!
Her whole room is Doctor Who crazy,
No such sight of a girly daisy!

She never used to be so bad,
But now she's making me mad!
At home she is so lazy,
And sometimes very crazy!

Kathryn Damoglou Pugh (11)
Ivy Lane Primary School, Chippenham

Lemons

Lemons in cakes
Lemons in drinks
Lemons are everywhere
All you have to do is think.

Lemon sweets in sweet shops
And lemon on your pancake
Lemons are citrusy
They liven up your taste buds
Bouncing in your mouth.

I love the taste of lemon sweets
When you put them in your mouth
That lovely citrus-like taste bubbling on your tongue
Mmm I can taste lemon right now!

Chloe Sheppard (10)
Ivy Lane Primary School, Chippenham

Seasons

Now here comes the spring,
All the flowers come out,
Listening to the birds sing,
Now here comes the spring!

Next is the summer,
It is boiling hot,
I wish it was winter,
Here is the summer!

The autumn is here,
The leaves falling off the trees,
The trees are dying, oh no, oh no, oh no,
The autumn is here!

The coldest season of the year,
The snow falling on the ground,
I'm so glad the heating is here,
The coldest season of year!

Chloe Jagger (10)
Ivy Lane Primary School, Chippenham

The Super Computer

Twenty thousand men it took,
But it's finished now,
Twenty thousand men it took,
To build the super computer.

Twenty thousand years it took
But it's working now,
Twenty thousand years it took,
To build the super computer.

Someone bought it at once
And tried to turn it on,
What a waste of money;
It blew up!

Neil Knight (10)
Ivy Lane Primary School, Chippenham

The Stream Monster

The stream looks like a strip of dusty blue silk.
You can hear it flowing and crashing off the bank.
You can see people sinking in its sand.
You can see fish and crabs swimming in it.
You can hear the birds flying overhead
And the leaves rustling in the wind.
But what I like best is the way its monster
Pulls you down under and you are gone for evermore!

Tuesday Blade Jeffries (10)
Ivy Lane Primary School, Chippenham

Boy Racers

Wheels spinning
Lights beaming
Exhaust smoking like a fire
Tyres screeching
Paintwork shimmering in the mist
Neon lights twinkling like the stars
Vroom vroom . . .

Dominic Biddle (10)
Ivy Lane Primary School, Chippenham

Guess What?

Slow walker
Plant eater
Slime maker
Shell user
Plant killer
Home mover
Trail leaver
Bird feeder
What am I?

A: Snail.

Josh Scott (10)
Ivy Lane Primary School, Chippenham

Silver Sorceress

The moon
Silver sorceress from the clouds
The moon
Shining from her throne up high

The moon
Sister of the sun
The moon
Glittering in her cloak of sky

The moon
She reigns over darkness
The moon
Lying on her bed of stars

The moon
Queen of all night
The moon
Mighty ruler from afar

The moon
Sparkling in all her glory
The moon
A sign of freedom

The moon
A lake of silver blood
The moon
In the night she will come

The moon
A light to those who cannot see
The moon
A shimmering glow

The moon
A gleaming halo
The moon
Though sister, sunlight is her foe

The moon
Dawn is her path of thorns
She rises at dusk
Only to fall at morn.

Eloise McAllister (10)
Kingswood Primary School, Wotton-under-Edge

The Glories Of Winter

Winter comes once a year,
It's very cold and the sky is clear.

The trees have no leaves,
They're all plain and bold,
My nose and my fingers are extremely cold.

My feet are like icebergs
With extra ice,
Which is really, really, really not nice.

So out come the thick socks,
The hat and the scarf
That will keep me warm, I'm sure of that.

So we light up the fire,
I sit at night,
Slopped in the chair with the red firelight.

My cheeks are aglow and my toes are like toast,
I can stretch out my feet
And I fall fast asleep.

Freya Ball (10)
Kingswood Primary School, Wotton-under-Edge

Friendship

F riends are always there for you.
R elying on you, gaining your trust.
I f you think you're alone it turns out you never are.
E ven if you argue it turns out alright in the end.
N ever ever will you be alone.
D on't ever break forever, you'll always be together.
S uper friends are always great!
H elp is always there when you need it.
I n different ways your friends will appear.
P lease stay friends or you won't be happy.

Victoria Copeland (10)
Kingswood Primary School, Wotton-under-Edge

Dogs

Dogs are big and dogs are small,
Almost any size at all.
They can fetch a big red ball,
They even come when you call.

Dogs go *woof* and dogs go *yap,*
Hardly ever take a nap.
They can sit upon your lap
And when they're good you can clap.

Chloe Moss (9)
Kingswood Primary School, Wotton-under-Edge

Home

H ome is where you hang your hearts
O h so happy and joyful
M aking cakes and having fun
E njoying with all the family.

Jennifer Smith (10)
Kingswood Primary School, Wotton-under-Edge

Evacuees - A Haiku

What should we expect?
Sadness is running through me.
Fire is around me.

Kathryn Price (10)
Longlevens Junior School, Longlevens

Pumpkin - Haiku

Pumpkins are scary
They have different faces
I love Hallowe'en.

Alice Loveday (10)
Longlevens Junior School, Longlevens

War - Haiku

War is frightening
Bombs drop on people's houses
My daddy's fighting.

Sarah Milne (10)
Longlevens Junior School, Longlevens

Blitz - Haiku

Bombs falling loudly
Buildings destroyed rapidly
Shelters full of fear.

Laura Thomas (10)
Longlevens Junior School, Longlevens

Moon - Haiku

Its craters glow up
It shines in the dark black sky
Covered in glitter.

Georgina Parry (10)
Longlevens Junior School, Longlevens

Blitz - Haiku

A fiery bomb
Massive lightning storm attacks
Anxious pilots cry.

Jack Hughes (10)
Longlevens Junior School, Longlevens

Moon - Haiku

The huge moon haunts me
Full moon rises up and shines
The moon is watching.

George Tirel (10)
Longlevens Junior School, Longlevens

Ghost - Haiku

A white cloud drifts by
The white sheet scaring children
White smoke whirling high.

Muazin Asad (10)
Longlevens Junior School, Longlevens

Moon - Haiku

Shimmering moon shines,
The bright moon stares out blankly,
The moon disappears.

Alexander Bates (10)
Longlevens Junior School, Longlevens

Pumpkin - Haiku

Pumpkins are scary
Flaming eyes watch over me
Candles flickering.

Elizabeth Willett (10)
Longlevens Junior School, Longlevens

Battlefields - Haiku

Sight of destruction
A gun and tank concoction
A fatal junction.

Dominic Trott (10)
Longlevens Junior School, Longlevens

Pumpkin - Haiku

An orange pumpkin
Beware a pumpkin is loose
A rolling pumpkin.

Harry Bevins (11)
Longlevens Junior School, Longlevens

Blitz - Haiku

An exploding bomb.
The people are terrified.
Bombs crush their houses.

Toby Lawrence (11)
Longlevens Junior School, Longlevens

War - Haiku

The dreadful world war
Destructive as a minefield
Countries to rubble.

Robert Grainger (10)
Longlevens Junior School, Longlevens

Hallowe'en - Haiku

Children dressing up
Trick or treaters knock on doors
Pumpkins stare at me.

Emma Cahill (10)
Longlevens Junior School, Longlevens

Hallowe'en - Haiku

Spine chilling shadows
Kids' screams echo through my head
Rustling in bushes.

Molly Geddes (10)
Longlevens Junior School, Longlevens

Ghost - Haiku

We see them at night,
White shimmering bright like kites,
In the air to scare.

Kieran Hayward (10)
Longlevens Junior School, Longlevens

Battlefields - Haiku

Battlefields blazing.
Mad blasting rapid firing.
Chaotic madness.

Sam Gabb (11)
Longlevens Junior School, Longlevens

Vampires - Haiku

Their fangs suck red blood
Wearing a black leather cape
Asleep in coffins.

Joe Richardson (10)
Longlevens Junior School, Longlevens

Werewolf - Haiku

Werewolves are deadly
Pierce through all the victims' throats
Howling at the moon.

Danny McCarthy (10)
Longlevens Junior School, Longlevens

Bullies

Bullies are normally nasty and large.
If you make them mad they may charge.
Bullies are always naughty and mean,
The most unkind people you've ever seen.

Bullies kick, bullies punch,
Then they steal food from your lovely lunch
And while you're crying they're very rude,
They don't yell 'sorry' they're not in the mood.

When the bully is around we don't lurk about,
That just makes him scream and shout,
Bullies are dishonest they always lie,
I wouldn't listen to them if you were I.

Megan Hunt (8)
Longlevens Junior School, Longlevens

Anger

Anger is hot, red as red as a fierce, erupting volcano.
Anger looks like a huge flaming fire.
Anger smells like a smoky bonfire.
Anger tastes like smelly burning oil.
Anger feels like a burning hot cup of tea poured down your back.
Anger sounds like an exploding Spitfire.
Anger reminds me of my annoying sister.

Matthew Lacey (9)
Manor Court Primary School, Chard

Happiness

Happiness looks like red roses in a see-through vase.
Happiness sounds like children laughing in the park.
Happiness tastes like strawberry-flavoured chocolate
Covered in dark chocolate.
Happiness smells like juicy fruit fresh from the trees.
Happiness feels like smooth beds just been made.
Colours of happiness are red, green, yellow and blue.
Happiness reminds me of a beautiful rainbow.

Jessica Kelly (9)
Manor Court Primary School, Chard

Happiness

Happiness is like the sound of children playing,
Happiness tastes like lovely chocolate,
Happiness feels like a soft teddy,
Happiness is the colour of baby blue,
Happiness is the smell of fresh flowers,
Happiness reminds me of my family,
Happiness looks like a smiley face.

Sophie Baker (10)
Manor Court Primary School, Chard

Love

Love sounds like a romantic guitar.
Love tastes like melted Galaxy chocolate.
Love smells like fresh air and lovely perfume.
Love is glittery shining roses.
Love is like red roses swishing.
Love feels like silk swirling.

Tiffany Watson (10)
Manor Court Primary School, Chard

Romance

Romance is like a loving love heart.
Romance is like a glowing heart.
Romance is red.
Romance is like a beautiful girl with some sweet flowers.
Romance is solid and can't break.
Romance is like sweet music.
Romance is
Love.

Tilly Porthouse (9)
Manor Court Primary School, Chard

Anger

Anger is red like fire
Anger looks like my mum when she is really mad

Anger smells like melting cherry

Anger tastes like a hot pepper

Anger feels like sun
Anger sounds like army men marching
Anger reminds me of the war.

Katherine Hall-Roberts (9)
Manor Court Primary School, Chard

Anger

Anger is red and blue mixed together
It looks like six volcanoes cracking
It smells like loads of burnt trees
Anger tastes like eating rocks
It feels like wanting to punch someone
It sounds like a big storm
Anger reminds me of a nightmare.

Kelsey Skinner (9)
Manor Court Primary School, Chard

When Happy Was Sad

Happiness is yellow like hot summer days.
Sadness is blue like cold rocky oceans.

Happiness tastes like a beautiful barbeque.
Sadness smells like dripping tears.

Happiness sounds like children playing happily in the sun.
Sadness sounds like screeching souls.

Happiness feels like people laughing.
Sadness feels like people crying.

Jake Crump (9)
Manor Court Primary School, Chard

When Anger Was Red

Anger is a red hot volcano.
It looks like a big red hot fire.
it smells like a red cherry melting.
It tastes like a red hot pepper.
It feels like a red balloon popping.
Anger sounds like an elephant stamping around.
It reminds me of a big red and green cherry.

Kirsty McQueen (9)
Manor Court Primary School, Chard

Happiness

Happiness is a colour like red and purple.
Happiness looks like lots of flowers.
Happiness smells like burgers cooking.
Happiness tastes like my friend.
Happiness feels like my cat on me.
Happiness sounds like my dad's bike.
Happiness reminds me of being in Year 4.

Rheannon Payne (10)
Manor Court Primary School, Chard

Emotion Poem

Anger is red like a red-hot balloon.

Anger looks like a red pepper.
Anger smells like a red flamingo.

Anger tastes like red peppers.
Anger feels like a hot and cold microwave.

Anger sounds like a trumpet.
Anger reminds me of a face.

Tianna Swain (10)
Manor Court Primary School, Chard

Emotion Poem

Nature is like the green grass
Nature looks like the seaweed
Nature is like the pongy smell of a fish
Nature tastes like ripe bananas
Nature feels like the sea crashing on me
Nature sounds like the trees waving in the air
Nature reminds me of the fresh air.

Daniel Brown (9)
Manor Court Primary School, Chard

Anger

Anger is red like fire
Anger looks like an exploding volcano
Anger smells like a petrol tank
Anger tastes like hot chilli
Anger feels like the sun
Anger sounds like firing guns
Anger reminds me of a car crash.

Samuel Hall (9)
Manor Court Primary School, Chard

Being Alone

Being alone is like being trapped in a place that no one knows.
It tastes like a tear from someone's eyes!
It smells like smoke from someone's house!
Being alone is a very dark colour,
Like black mixed with dark green.
It sounds like someone's crying and asking for help!
It feels like a fear that makes you scared!
Being alone reminds you of your happy times and your lonely times.
It's like you're imaging your future and past!

Charlene Pablo (10)
Manor Court Primary School, Chard

Happiness

Happiness is yellow.
Happiness looks like the sun.
Happiness sounds like a musical instrument.
Happiness smells like fresh air.
Happiness tastes like chocolate.
It reminds me of a sunny day.

Ellis Lewis (9)
Manor Court Primary School, Chard

Anger

Anger looks like an erupting volcano.
Anger looks like a spitting snake.
Anger sounds like a dog growling.
Anger smells like mouldy cheese.
Anger smells like wood burning.
Anger feels like a prickly hedgehog!

Liam Willcocks (9)
Manor Court Primary School, Chard

Happiness!

Happiness sounds like children playing,
It tastes like gummy bears,
It smells like freshly baked cookies
And is the colour of a mermaid's hair,
It feels like a roller coaster ride where you never have to get off.
Happiness reminds me of my mum,
Happiness is me!

Mary Smith (10)
Manor Court Primary School, Chard

Happiness!

Happiness sounds like children playing.
Happiness looks like a big fat chocolate cake.
Happiness tastes like strawberry ice cream.
Happiness feels like the big yellow sun.
Happiness smells like a big pink rose.
Happiness reminds me of the beach.
Happiness is the colour yellow.

Laura Watts (10)
Manor Court Primary School, Chard

Hate

Hate is dark red like blood,
Hate feels like an egg sliding through your fingers,
Hate sounds like a bad drum in your ear,
Hate tastes like a rat dying,
Hate reminds me of a volcano just about to erupt,
Hate looks like dark red blood,
Hate smells like burning petrol.

Amy Blanksby (10)
Manor Court Primary School, Chard

Anger

Anger's like a volcano erupting before your eyes.
Anger is like being ruler of the world.
Anger is like horror smacking you.
Anger sounds like thunder haunting you.
Anger reminds me of my nan dying because I was not there for her.
Anger looks like sacrifice.
Anger feels like something's broken inside you.
Anger tastes like the world is going to explode.
Anger is your feelings. Your feeling is your anger.

Alfie Arnold (10)
Manor Court Primary School, Chard

Love

Love feels like lips rubbing up against each other.
Love looks like one watery rose.
Love smells like two fresh roses.
Love looks like really light pink.
Love sounds like two people kissing.

Daniel Mason (10)
Manor Court Primary School, Chard

Love Is In The Air

Love looks like strawberry
Love tastes like juicy red apples
Love smells like chocolate
Love sounds like love music
Love feels like big red hearts
The colour of love is bright red
Love reminds me of my nan!

Shannon Clark (10)
Manor Court Primary School, Chard

,adness

Sadness reminds me of people suffering in other countries.
Sadness is blue like the deep blue sea.
Sadness feels like you're lonely.
Sadness sounds like people crying.
Sadness smells like water because of tears.
Sadness tastes like a banana because bananas are droopy.
Sadness looks like an animal in pain.

Christopher Goodhew (10)
Manor Court Primary School, Chard

Love

Love feels like Cupid has shot you with an arrow.
Love looks like pink and red hearts.
Love smells like strawberries and cream.
Love sounds like kisses - two lips touching.
Love tastes like strawberry sweets.

Jordi Morgan (10)
Manor Court Primary School, Chard

Love

Love is like a pink huge balloon.
Love looks like a beautiful sun.
Love smells like red roses.
Love reminds me of pink gigantic marshmallows.
Love sounds like angels singing loud.
Love feels like the world.
Love tastes like melted chocolate.

Matthew Hill (10)
Manor Court Primary School, Chard

Sadness

Sadness is blue like the deep blue sea.
Sadness feels like you're dying.
Sadness smells like tears from a dying person.
Sadness sounds like a dying breath.
Sadness tastes like blood.
Sadness looks like people rolled up in a ball.

Daniel Lee Smith (11)
Manor Court Primary School, Chard

Fear

Fear is black like a dark night sky,
Fear looks like a deep dark hole,
Fear sounds like the bang of fireworks,
Fear feels like a rotten banana,
Fear tastes like a mouldy biscuit,
Fear smells like burning toast,
Fear reminds me of thunder.

Shannon Baker (10)
Manor Court Primary School, Chard

Love

Love is pink like candyfloss
Love smells like a bouquet of flowers
Love feels like an enormous marshmallow
Love tastes like melted chocolate
Love sounds like angels singing
Love looks like a giant heart
Love reminds me of my PS2.

Connor Morgan (10)
Manor Court Primary School, Chard

adness

Sadness is light blue like an early morning sky,
Sadness sounds like people crying all around me,
Sadness tastes like a really sour sweet,
Sadness smells like salty water,
Sadness feels like nothing can go right,
Sadness reminds me of a world without happiness or love.

Laura Hall (10)
Manor Court Primary School, Chard

Sadness

Sadness tastes like pickle.
Sadness feels like chlorine in your eyes.
Sadness looks like people crying.
Sadness sounds like death.
Sadness smells like rotten bananas.
Sadness is purple like plums.
Sadness reminds me of a puppy being put to sleep.

Amy Laura Gage (11)
Manor Court Primary School, Chard

Love

Love is pink like an enormous marshmallow.
Love feels like a fluffy puppy.
Love tastes like fresh strawberries.
Love sounds like angels singing.
Love looks like a heart shaped cloud.
Love smells like roses.
Love reminds me of the calm ocean.

Christopher Haughton (10)
Manor Court Primary School, Chard

Love Poem

Love is light pink, like a giant marshmallow.
Love looks like a heart-shaped cloud.
Love tastes like chocolate.
Love sounds like angels singing.
Love smells like roses.
Love reminds me of flowers.
Love feels like a soft blanket.

Hannah Pearce (10)
Manor Court Primary School, Chard

Hate

Hate is deep red like Manchester United.
Hate feels like nastiness.
Hate smells like bright red blood.
Hate sounds like shouting.
Hate reminds me of sour grapes.
Hate tastes like strawberries and cream.
Hate looks like big spiders.

Jordan Totterdell (10)
Manor Court Primary School, Chard

Sadness

Sadness is blue like the sea.
Sadness feels like you are lonely.
Sadness smells like tears.
Sadness sounds like people dying.
Sadness tastes like Brussels sprouts.
Sadness looks like people starving.

Ashley Briant (10)
Manor Court Primary School, Chard

₊te

₊ate is red like the Devil,
Hate sounds like an angry lion's roar,
Hate looks like a blood red sky,
Hate feels like walking over broken glass,
Hate tastes like mouldy cream,
Hate smells like strong gone-off cheese,
Hate reminds me of someone's face red with fury!

Wednesday Watson (11)
Manor Court Primary School, Chard

Fear

Fear is black like a dark sky.
Fear tastes like sour apples.
Fear reminds me of a dark tunnel.
Fear smells like an old room.
Fear sounds like banging in your ears.
Fear looks like a dark hole in the ground.
Fear feels like pins and needles in your arms.

Warren Lewis (10)
Manor Court Primary School, Chard

Hate!

Hate smells like petrol,
Hate looks like deep red blood,
Hate sounds like a balloon popping,
Hate is red like fire,
Hate feels like sharp needles,
Hate tastes of toads' wee,
Hate reminds me of a steaming cauldron!

Alice Fenner (10)
Manor Court Primary School, Chard

Lilac And Silver

Lilac is my favourite colour,
Lilac flowers smell the best,
Lilac makes me feel calm
And especially makes me rest!
Silver makes me feel happy,
Silver reminds me of my silver medal,
Silver reminds me of my mum's silver car,
Go on Mum step on the pedal!

Alana Hake (8)
Manor Court Primary School, Chard

Anger

Anger is red like a volcano.
Anger feels like taking over the world.
Anger tastes like hot chilli.
Anger smells like rotting carrots.
Anger sounds like a tornado.
Anger reminds me of an earthquake.
Anger looks like a screaming train.

Louise Mackenzie (10)
Manor Court Primary School, Chard

Fear

Fear is black like outer space,
Fear tastes like sour apples
Fear reminds me of a dark tunnel,
Fear smells like an old room,
Fear looks like a black spider,
Fear feels like pins and needles,
Fear sounds like banging in your ears.

Jess Mathieson (10)
Manor Court Primary School, Chard

Anger

Anger sounds like screaming, screeching abuse.
Anger tastes like stolen words spat on and demolished.
Anger smells like a burnt delicacy wasting away in a spit roast fire.
Anger is a deep red or a dark night sky.
Anger looks like a steel jaw slightly ajar.
Anger feels like a burning rage or desire.
Anger reminds me of crying after an undeniable, horrible incident.

Sophie Holloway (11)
Manor Court Primary School, Chard

Pink

Pink is the thought of a baby smiling to me.
Pink is the sound of babies laughing.
Pink is the animal elephant, neighing.
Pink is the taste of cherries, all sweet for me.
Pink is the book 'Puppy Love' that barks all the time.
The pink cosy toes of the babies' feet squelching in pink paint on
my bedroom wall.

Pink makes me happy.

Zoe Molesworth (9)
Manor Court Primary School, Chard

Red

Red is the colour of danger and anger,
It reminds me of tae kwon-do belts,
It reminds me of devils and broken roller coasters
And sometimes it scares me to death!
Sometimes it causes danger,
Sometimes it makes you angry,
But in either way red is the colour of scared!

Niamh Rodgers (8)
Manor Court Primary School, Chard

Purple

My favourite colour is purple
Because my mum's coat is purple
And I love purple because of the swish, swash flowers.
Purple is clambering flowers up a fence.
Purple is calm,
It tastes like grapes.
Purple is relaxing.

Tyrone Payne (8)
Manor Court Primary School, Chard

Yellow

Yellow makes you feel warm inside
Yellow makes you feel peaceful and happy
Yellow makes you feel hungry
Yellow makes you feel loved
Yellow makes you buy yellow flowers
Yellow makes you feel worried
Yellow makes you feel cosy
Yellow makes you buy bananas.

Amy Barrett (8)
Manor Court Primary School, Chard

Fear

Fear is as black as space.
Fear is like gritting teeth.
Fear smells like burnt popcorn.
Fear sounds like drums in my ear.
Fear feels like a solid wall.
Fear looks like an empty mind.
Fear reminds me of a hissing cat.
Fear tastes like burnt pizza.

Ben James Grime (10)
Manor Court Primary School, Chard

Hunger

Hunger is like food that doesn't want to be eaten.
Hunger is like food that sprints away.
Hunger is like people in Africa with no food.

Tony Redman (10)
Manor Court Primary School, Chard

White

White reminds me of polar bears
Polar bears are bright
White is my favourite colour
Because white makes me happy and cold
White makes me energetic.

Leonel Cruz (8)
Manor Court Primary School, Chard

Hate

Hate is red like the stop light.
It reminds me of witches' blood.
It tastes like mushy peas.
It sounds like a loud drum in your ears.

Sophie White (10)
Manor Court Primary School, Chard

Red

Red is love
Red is roses
Red is lovely
Red is exciting
Red is hot.

Lewis Day (8)
Manor Court Primary School, Chard

White

White is a happy colour
Because it looks like the sky.
White is the colour like a floppy white rabbit.
White is my favourite colour,
It makes me feel happy.

Cristine Pablo (8)
Manor Court Primary School, Chard

Red

Makes me feel fiery,
Makes me feel powerful.
Red tastes like strawberries and tomato ketchup.
Red makes me feel joyful
When I see red stripes for a kite.

Abigail Trott (8)
Manor Court Primary School, Chard

Red

Red is angry like a fire.
Red is blood pumping down your body.
Red is a strawberry which tastes so good.
Red is cosy just like a sofa.

Fraser Porthouse (8)
Manor Court Primary School, Chard

Red

Red is angry.
Red is fire.
Red is powerful.
I like the colour red.

Jack Cruise (9)
Manor Court Primary School, Chard

Red

Red makes me angry because it is hot like a hot chilli pepper.
Red is sometimes joyful because it reminds you of the Roman shields.
It reminds you of the shiny glimmering apple.
Red makes me feel warm inside.

Kira Bellamy (8)
Manor Court Primary School, Chard

Blue

Blue is bright like the sky,
The taste of blueberries.
Happiness is the sky and a garden of blue flowers.
It feels joyful and laughing.
Blue is fun.

Neil Parkes (9)
Manor Court Primary School, Chard

Red

Red feels like nice cushions.
Red tastes like tomato sauce.
Red is someone angry.
Red makes me think of fire.
Red looks like apples on a tree.

Jake Ripley (8)
Manor Court Primary School, Chard

Anger

Anger is red like a volcano
Anger looks like a red face
Anger smells like a red fire
Anger feels like a rook.

Liam Clark (9)
Manor Court Primary School, Chard

Gold

Gold makes me happy when I am cross.
Gold is sparkly like a sparkly star shining in the sky.
I love gold stuff.
I like gold because I have a gold pen.
Gold is a lovely colour in the world.

Chloe Rendell (8)
Manor Court Primary School, Chard

Yellow

Yellow is quiet and loved.
It makes you feel lovely and calm.
The garden is full of yellow flowers.
Just walk outside for the yellow brightness.

Kelly Burke (8)
Manor Court Primary School, Chard

Red

Anger is bright red.
Red tastes of tomatoes.
Red makes me feel cross.
Red is fire.
Red is blood.

Adam Walker (8)
Manor Court Primary School, Chard

Orange

Orange is the colour of hot sun.
Orange is a calm, loving colour.
It is my favourite colour!

Phoebe Earl (9)
Manor Court Primary School, Chard

Black

Black feels like a dark space inside and it makes you angry.
Black is like a storm,
Black bats and ants crawling,
Rain tumbles down.
Black is sad and worrying, it makes you scared
And dark clouds fill the air.

Dominic Lane (8)
Manor Court Primary School, Chard

Red

Red feels like devils!
Red is death!
Red knows blood!
Red tastes like sour sweets, tomatoes, strawberries
And red berries!
Red gets angry, stressed, furious and sad!
Red is fire and restful! *Ouch!*

James Parsons (8)
Manor Court Primary School, Chard

Pink

Pink feels like love.
Pink tastes like a strawberry.
Pink looks like a pink heart.
Pinks smells like pink roses.
Pink sounds like someone singing.
Pink makes me happy.

Kate Hall (8)
Manor Court Primary School, Chard

Lilac

Lilac is my favourite colour, it fills me with delight,
It looks like flowers blowing in the wind,
It tastes like sweet blueberries.
Lilac makes me feel fuzzy inside,
The last thing lilac does for me is wrap around me
Like a cosy, warm and fluffy blanket.

Lucy Bailey (8)
Manor Court Primary School, Chard

Relaxed

Relaxed is blue like watching the calm sea.
Relaxed is peace and quiet.
Relaxed is eating a plate of cheese.
Relaxed smells like fresh air.
Relaxed feels like nice ice cream.
Relaxed reminds me of sitting down.

Josh Totterdell (9)
Manor Court Primary School, Chard

Red

Red makes me angry.
Red tastes like jam.
Red smells like blood.
Red looks like roses.
Red is fire.
Red things remind me of when I'm angry.

Caitlin Grime (8)
Manor Court Primary School, Chard

Love!

Love is pink like a pin rose growing from a seed.
Love is like being more than a friend.
Love sounds like church bells ringing for a marriage.
Love tastes like someone giving another chocolates.
Love smells of lovely flowers.
Love feels like a soft fluffy love bear.
Love reminds me of a baby being born.

Mollie Briant (9)
Manor Court Primary School, Chard

Sadness

Sadness is cream.
It looks like melting ice cream.
It looks like a slithering slug.
It sounds like a cat crying.
It tastes like squashed tomatoes.
It smells like a horrible farm.
It feels like a wooden floor.
It reminds me of being alone.

Abbie Thompson (9)
Manor Court Primary School, Chard

Love

Love is like a pink rose.
Love is like being in Heaven.
Love sounds like roses.
It sounds like birds singing.
It tastes like chocolate ice cream.
It feels like fluffy clouds.
It reminds me of a loving boy.

Savanna Hall (10)
Manor Court Primary School, Chard

Liveliness

Liveliness is multicoloured like a shimmering bright rainbow.
Liveliness smells like a strawberry ice cream covered in hundreds
and thousands.
Liveliness tastes like a bar of truffle drowned in chocolate sauce.
Liveliness sounds like children opening their bright colourful
presents on Christmas morning.
Liveliness feels like a giant ball pit filled with thousands of balls.
Liveliness looks like newborn puppies cuddling up to their mothers.
Liveliness reminds me of jumping on my double bed with silk
white sheets.

Tiffany Zenda (9)
Manor Court Primary School, Chard

Love

Love is a soft red, like a red rose.
Love is like dreaming in your sleep.
Love sounds like wedding bells.
Love tastes like creamy chocolate mousse.
Love smells like sweet perfume.
Love feels like a moment of happiness.
Love reminds me of Romeo and Juliet.

Alice Hall (9)
Manor Court Primary School, Chard

Yellow

Yellow makes me feel happy.
Yellow makes me hungry.
I want to eat a banana.
Yellow is a light colour.

Daniel Da Silva (9)
Manor Court Primary School, Chard

Anger

Anger is like a bright burning fire.
Anger looks like red hot chilli peppers.
Anger tastes like rotten blue cheese.
Anger feels like damp brown, crunchy leaves.
Anger is dark like a haunted, gloomy house.
Anger is like the rough waves of the ocean.
Anger looks like an exploding volcano.
Anger reminds me of colourful exploding fireworks.
Anger reminds me of the rapid rain on the cold damp conservatory.

Kylie Jeynes (9)
Manor Court Primary School, Chard

Hopeful

Hopeful is yellow like the sun rising up into the sky,
Hopeful sounds like joy and happiness in the dark blue sea
And it tastes like a yummy strawberry cheesecake in the clouds,
It smells like yummy cheese,
It feels lovely like a real comfy cushion,
It reminds me of having a good night's sleep in my bed.

Hannah Lord (9)
Manor Court Primary School, Chard

Forgiving

Forgiving is purple like a purple flower in bloom.
Forgiving looks like people shaking hands.
Forgiving tastes like sweet hot cocoa.
Forgiving smells like daffodils.
Forgiving feels like a fluffy cushion.
Forgiving reminds me of friends.

Courtney Wyatt (9)
Manor Court Primary School, Chard

Love

Love is pink like someone kissing on the lips.
Love is like a baby being born.
Love sounds like someone kissing on the lips.
Love tastes like lovely sweet things.
Love smells like a romantic dinner.
It feels like a time once in a lifetime.
It reminds me of when we first met!

Leanne Grimstead (9)
Manor Court Primary School, Chard

Love

Love is pink.
Love is like a teddy bear.
Love is like a fluffy, soft and warm pillow.
Love sounds like a twinkling silver star.
Love tastes like sweet chocolate.
Love smells like cream.
Love feels like angels' wings.
Love reminds me of hearts.

Mae Daniels (9)
Manor Court Primary School, Chard

Red!

Red is angry, it is very hurtful.
It tastes like sour apple.
Red is furious and makes me scream with anger.
It feels like fire.
Red is fun!

Emily Bilboe (8)
Manor Court Primary School, Chard

Love

Love is pink like a cute puppy being born.
Love smells like a beautiful perfume.
Love tastes like a delicious chocolate cake.
Love feels like a beautiful snake's shimmering skin.
Love reminds me of a racing rocket soaring into space.
Love reminds me of a pink heart filled with caring thoughts.
Love is like a majestic parade in my mind.

Rebecca Orchard (9)
Manor Court Primary School, Chard

Love

Love is red like sweet, bright red roses.
Love smells like a big love heart-shaped box of chocolates.
Love tastes like freshly picked ripe raspberries.
Love feels like two smooth hands gently rubbing together.
Love sounds like calm and gentle music.
Love reminds me of my heart slowly and calmly beating.

Kirsty Robertson (9)
Manor Court Primary School, Chard

Cowardice

Cowardice is brown like chocolate.
Cowardice smells like cold soup.
Cowardice tastes like dirty washing.
Cowardice feels like lightning striking on a cold night.
Cowardice sounds like tears dropping on the kitchen floor.
Cowardice looks like a volcano dripping its last drops.
Cowardice reminds me of daisy cows.

Rhyann Watton (9)
Manor Court Primary School, Chard

Gold

Gold is tasty just like toffee.
Gold is warm just like coffee.
Gold is short and is not tall.
Gold is very tropical.

I like glitter when it's in gold
And an old gold car is to behold.
What looks very good in gold
Is a glittery book, even if it's old.

Gold makes me feel warm and bright,
It's like a blanket cosy and tight.
Gold . . . is the best . . . colour . . . ever!

James Woodcraft (8)
Manor Court Primary School, Chard

Grumpiness

Grumpiness is red like hot fire.
It smells like red-hot chilli.
The taste is like steamy water from a steamer.
It feels like concrete all lumpy and bumpy.
Grumpiness reminds me of people stamping around the place.

Ryan Board (9)
Manor Court Primary School, Chard

Fear

Fear is dark green like a frog leaping madly.
Fear smells like the inside of a volcano.
Fear tastes like hard ice cubes.
Fear sounds like a monster stomping madly.

Liam Board (9)
Manor Court Primary School, Chard

Love

Love is red like smooth roses.
Love smells of bright red raspberries.
Love tastes of juicy strawberries.
Love feels like your heart has exploded like an erupting volcano.
Love sounds like a heart is beating really fast.
Love reminds me of hot boiled sweets melting in my mouth.

Megan Curtis (9)
Manor Court Primary School, Chard

Excitement

Excitement is pink like brightly coloured flowers.
Excitement looks like flowering buds.
Excitement smells like blossoming trees.
Excitement tastes like chicken korma.
Excitement feels like soft dog fur.
Excitement sounds like Grease Lightning.
Excitement reminds me of happy holidays.

Elise Bradley (9)
Manor Court Primary School, Chard

Laughter

Laughter is multicoloured like a rainbow.
Laughter smells like freezing ice cream on the table.
It tastes like every animal's favourite food.
It feels like going on holiday to the beach.

Emily Boyland (9)
Manor Court Primary School, Chard

Fun

Fun is the feeling I have when I'm on my daddy's shoulders.
Fun is like leaves being blown in my face.
Fun is the lovely feeling of flying like a bird.
Fun smells like beautiful red roses.
Fun tastes like nice juicy apples.

Charlotte Davies (9)
Manor Court Primary School, Chard

Anger Poem

Anger is burning purple like something exploding.
Anger looks like a flower dying.
Anger smells like a fire going off.
Anger tastes like hot chilli peppers.
Anger feels like winter passing by.
Anger sounds like a screeching elephant.
Anger reminds me of blasting music.

Rebecca Black (9)
Manor Court Primary School, Chard

Ella The Elephant

Ella the elephant is really strong,
She's also very large,
But if you bother to wake her up
She will run and she will charge.

Vicky Matthews (8)
Manor Court Primary School, Chard

Happiness

Happiness tastes like sweets.
Happiness is the colour of bright, bright blue like curtains blocking
                                                      the light out.
Happiness smells nice like onions.
Happiness sounds like presents being unwrapped.
Happiness reminds me of eating sweets.
Happiness looks like a thousand pounds worth of sweets.

Harry Meggitt (10)
Manor Court Primary School, Chard

Love

Love sounds like a breeze flowing through the trees.
Love looks like a couple getting married in a church.
Love tastes like strawberry and cream freshly made.
Love feels like warm hearts beating very slowly but healthily.
Love smells like a rose just grown at home.
Love is the colour of a baby blue bridesmaid dress.
Love reminds me of a newborn puppy crying for its mum.

Kirsty Rendell (10)
Manor Court Primary School, Chard

Hunger

Hunger is the colour of red and blue.
Hunger tastes like a cheese pizza.
Hunger looks like a scoop of mash potato.
Hunger reminds you of the last time you ate something.
Hunger feels like a lump in your throat.
Hunger smells like a burning bonfire getting warmer.

Matthew Long (9)
Walton Primary School, Walton

Loneliness

Loneliness is like the colour of blue ice cubes, making you shiver.
Loneliness tastes like warm popcorn popping in your mouth.
Loneliness smells like salty tears making you want to cry.
Loneliness feels like global warming, you want to do something
but you can't.
Loneliness reminds me of a family breaking apart - making you sad.
Loneliness feels like a sharp pin pricking you, you want to scream!
Loneliness looks like a leaf on a tree with lots of friends then you fall
down and you are alone.

Erin McKenzie (9)
Walton Primary School, Walton

Happiness

Happiness tastes like fresh strawberries and cream topped
with icing sugar.
Happiness reminds me of somebody licking a lolly dripping down
their top.
Happiness smells like bacon frying in pan *mmmm!*
Happiness feels like ice cream melting on my tongue.

Alina Briscomb (9)
Walton Primary School, Walton

Sadness

Sadness feels like you're empty with no home and no friends at all.
Sadness reminds me of a poor thin, lost child, cold and hungry.
Sadness smells of gone-off milk, bitter and revolting.
Sadness is the colour of green sick.
Sadness tastes like warm cabbage *yuck!*
Sadness looks like a dead puppy.

Bethany Reece (9)
Walton Primary School, Walton

Cats Are Like Sofas

Cats are like sofas,
All shapes and sizes,
Lazing around all day long,
Squeaking and springy,
Some can be strong
And others weak,
But I like both of them soft and comfy.

They come home soft and furry,
Playful, a bounce in every spring,
Some have a worry
And some called Ming.

Then they get old and soon die out,
But still within memory,
Without a doubt,
Then there is an excuse to get a new one,
Which is just as important to me.

Georgina Buckner (10)
Walton Primary School, Walton

The Sun

The sun is like a lion
Bright golden yellow
But secretly short-tempered
Eating up the darkness
Just lying there all day
Slightly moving every second
But she brightens up the day.

And when she hears thunder
She hides behind a cloud
Then when she comes back out again
She does not make a sound
She simply smiles.

Francesca Fallows (10)
Walton Primary School, Walton

Hunger!

Hunger is multicoloured like a fresh rainbow inside your stomach.
Hunger tastes like a bitter acid on the inside of your throat.
Hunger looks like a big explosion of every single food you could ever imagine in all different shapes, sizes and colours.
Hunger reminds me of the biggest bowl you could ever think of that is just about ready to explode into a million pieces.
Hunger feels like you are empty and it makes you feel as if you don't want to move.
Hunger is a very, very dull smell that is like greasy fish and chips you have just brought home from the restaurant.

Charlotte Dearman (10)
Walton Primary School, Walton

In The Night

In my dreams
I see an elephant that's massive,
I see a dog that's loud,
I see a tiger that's speedy.

In my dreams
I meet a monster that's terrifying,
I meet a ninja turtle that's cool,
I meet a mummy that's weird.

In my dreams
I do superhero work that's muscular,
I do secret spy work that's crafty,
I do surfing that's done with pleasure,
That's what I do in my dreams.

Jay Daniells (8)
Walton Primary School, Walton

Loneliness

Loneliness feels like your heart is going to pop out of your mouth -
It is a lump in your throat and it feels like you've lost all your money.
Loneliness is orange and white, all plain and boring.
Loneliness is a horrid smell, it's like a sour flower, composting
Loneliness is a taste that is not pleasant, it tastes like rotten
strawberries with salt.
Loneliness looks like a deserted wood with leaves crunching under
your feet.
Loneliness reminds me of the bad times, what does loneliness
remind you of?

Sophie Purchase (9)
Walton Primary School, Walton

Loneliness

Loneliness looks like a boring black midnight sky.
Loneliness smells like rotten cabbage, all brown and burnt.
Loneliness tastes like blue cheese that has gone all mouldy.
Loneliness reminds me of creepy-crawlies buzzing around my head.
Loneliness feels like crisps that are wet and soggy.
Loneliness has the colour of really dark red like the inside of a
witch's cloak.

Sam Vowles (10)
Walton Primary School, Walton

Loneliness

Loneliness is like a friend not being there for you.
Loneliness is the colour of cold and icy mornings.
Loneliness smells like sour chicken thrown in the dustbin.
Loneliness looks like a sad face.
Loneliness reminds you of a tear dropping down your face.
Loneliness feels like a bad day at school.

Chloe Dykes (10)
Walton Primary School, Walton

Loneliness

Loneliness is white like melting ice cubes cracking in my head.
Loneliness smells like burnt marshmallows that are not springy
                    anymore when toasted on the fire.
Loneliness feels like sharp dragon's prickles that don't prick anymore.
Loneliness tastes like a bad breath leaf and rotten chilli peppers.
Loneliness looks bare and pitch-black with no one inside of it.
Loneliness reminds me of a room that has nobody in it, just plain old
                    lights with smelly spiders and dusty cobwebs.

Karla White (10)
Walton Primary School, Walton

Darkness

Darkness is as black as night.
Darkness tastes like a bitter tomato freshly picked.
Darkness looks like a horrible ghost swooping through an old barn.
Darkness reminds me of giant spiders in a haunted house.
Darkness feels like an icy cold wind through an open window.
Darkness smells like a big forest fire spitting out sparks.
Darkness is scary!

Alfred Beaty (9)
Walton Primary School, Walton

Calmness

Calmness feels like a river flowing gently through the woods.
Calmness is a purple gem dancing in the moonlight.
Calmness smells like a freshly baked Yorkshire pudding.
Calmness looks like a bright star in the sky.
Calmness reminds me of my family that loves me.
Calmness tastes like a scoop of cold ice cream.

Lauren Baker (9)
Walton Primary School, Walton

Happiness

Happiness is like a bubbly feeling inside my heart
ready to burst with joy.
Happiness tastes like an explosion of sherbet trickling down my throat
with a fantastic taste that reminds me of a joyful moment.
Happiness is the colour of summer sun that is bright
and makes me jump with joy.
Happiness smells like a bunch of roses
that have been freshly picked from a wood or garden.
Happiness reminds me of a garden with my friends and family
talking happily surrounded by a bed of flowers.
Happiness looks like a happy rainbow across the beautiful blue sky.

Hannah Toal (9)
Walton Primary School, Walton

Sadness

Sadness feels like your heart sinking as a stone to your stomach.
Sadness looks like a misty figure of joy painfully turning its back
on your soul.
Sadness tastes like salt or gone-off milk.
Sadness is like a pastel blue space of depression.
Sadness is too hard to bear.

Katherine Hubbuck (10)
Walton Primary School, Walton

A Little Child Is Like A Monkey!

A little child's like a monkey
Clever and cute
Two hands, two feet
Banana eater, tree climber
Very cheeky and full of mischief
With long brown hair and a long brown tail.

Abbie Robins (10)
Walton Primary School, Walton

Scary

Scary tastes like cold, wet and sour, getting more bitter hour by hour.
Scary looks as black as night, it's so dark it will give you a fright.
Scary gives reminders of death and unhealthiness,
See it too much it will make you feel nauseous.
Scary feels icy, hairy and weird, this feeling is so often feared.
Scary smells plain, horrible and mouldy, get too close,
It could be faulty.
Scary has the colours of black and white,
Its darkest fear is at night.

Izzy Hicks (10)
Walton Primary School, Walton

Fun

Fun is when you play and play with your best friend.
Fun is like a multicoloured rainbow exploding inside my stomach.
Fun tastes like mashed potato on a winter evening.
Fun reminds me of my family and my pet rabbit called Snowy.
Fun looks like a park on a spring morning.
Fun is fun.

Olivia Nelson (9)
Walton Primary School, Walton

The Morning

Birds singing, alarm clocks ringing call me out of bed,
Splishing, sploshing face needs washing,
Then dry my sleepyhead,
Down the stairs pitter-patter,
Toaster pops, teacups clatter,
Breakfast sizzling on my plate.

Daisy Huxter (10)
Walton Primary School, Walton

The Seasons

I walked to school on Monday morning, feeling a chill stream down
my spine,

The sky is grey, the air is crisp,
And I'm running out of time.
But my legs are stiff, my fingers numb, as my watch ticks on
my wrist,

The snow tickles me on my nose,
As I crunch my way through the frost,
And I'm sure that when I get to school I'll be well and truly froze!

I walked to school on Monday morning, feeling bursts of fresh air fill
my nose,

The trees above me are full of buds and tiny baby birds,
A dazzling sunrise lights the sky, but I'm still in a sleepy doze.

I walked to school on Monday morning, feeling the warm sunrise on
my face,

The bouncy grass beneath my feet is filled with pretty flowers,
But as I walk, I start to sweat under the rays of the sun's hot powers,
So I head for some shade under the green luscious trees,
But there's a buzzing on the flowers, oh no, it's the bees!

I walked to school on Monday morning, feeling a leaf get caught
in my shoe,

The cold is here and the trees are bare,
And a crunching sound can now be heard,
The sound is the leaves, golden and brown, crumpled and old.

These are the seasons, for we all know,
In winter plants die, but in the spring they grow.

Georgia Corrigan (10)
Walton Primary School, Walton

School Bus

It's 7 in the morning I've just woken up,
Inside's full of rubbish, crisp bags and cups.
All this from the children who ride me to school,
Or go for a swim at Strode swimming pool.

I breakfast on diesel, the best of my treats,
Then out comes the oil can to fix squeaky seats.
Here comes my driver all dressed up so smart,
It's 7.45 now so let's make a start.

I've almost arrived at the very first stop,
Let's hope they are nice or they'll be for the chop.
Now onwards I'm speeding towards that school gate,
Yes! Another success I'm early not late.

3.30, oh no! I must drive them home,
Those chattering children do nothing but moan.
4.50, I've finished but tomorrow's ahead,
My tyres are so tired I'm off to my bed.

Charlie France (10)
Walton Primary School, Walton

My Teddies

I took four teddies to the woods one day,
We had a party picnic, we drank lots of lemonade.
The food was delicious, we had fish and chips,
All of us played teddy bear tag in the woods,
Then the four teddies and me went for a walk,
We saw beautiful trees and the sun was shining.
The birds were chirping and the sky was blue,
Then it got dark and it started to rain,
We all went home.

Chloe Pitman (8)
Walton Primary School, Walton

My Pet Rats!

I change their food daily,
We rinse their water too.

Together we clean them out,
I really love and care for them.

I let them run around,
I play and get them out.

Daisy is a fatty ratty,
She sits in her beds,
Eats all the food,
Her favourite is roast chicken.

Winnie is a skinny rat,
She used to be brown,
But now she's pink and warm,
I let her crawl all over me.

I really love them very much,
Sniffly, snuffly, sniff, sniff!

Grace Hegarty (8)
Walton Primary School, Walton

My Holiday

I went on holiday to Florida,
It turned so hot and humid,
I went to a few theme parks,
I should have said all,
Every night we would go out,
Posh restaurants it was,
I stayed up very late,
So my holiday is over,
It was so much fun.

Abigail Lockyer (9)
Walton Primary School, Walton

Lightning

Lightning is like a cheetah,
Bright silver stripe zooming across the sky,
Sneezing all over the enormous soggy ground below.

The lightning takes a picture,
Animals hiding nervously in the forest,
The dark houses lay lifeless,
The trees howl in terror.

The roots cling on for dear life,
The people surround the candle praying to be saved,
The cars put their headlights on full beam.

Francesca Chinnock (10)
Walton Primary School, Walton

My Friend Harry

He has a nose as red as a tomato,
Hair as brown as chocolate,
Eyes like shining diamonds
And lips as cold as ice.

His arms are as long and gangly as Mr Tickles,
His ears are as yellow as lemons,
He has legs as weak as a newborn lamb
And he has a face as white as the moon.

He has feet as smelly as Stilton
And hands as spotty as chickenpox.

And people think I'm strange!

Liberty Bingham (10)
Walton Primary School, Walton

The Carnival

Bright lights, bright costumes,
People laughing, people dancing,
Loud music thumping as the floats go by.
Donation buckets carried past, money chattering inside.
Children pushing through the crowd, try to get the best view.
Then, the last float is chugging slowly down the road,
And the carnival has come to an end.

Hannah Corrigan (9)
Walton Primary School, Walton

What I Can Do In A Day

Wake up, get dressed,
Eat my breakfast, make a mess,
Tidy up, put shoes on,
Wash my face and hands,
Make myself look grand,
Go to school, feeling cool,
Crunchy munch, munch,
Have my snack and lunch,
Get home, have tea,
Watch a programme on TV,
Brush my teeth, go to bed,
Dream all night sleepyhead.

Katherine Fallows (9)
Walton Primary School, Walton

Ibiza

Shops are boring or nice,
The food was yummy too,
The drinks were refreshing as well as the food,
The water park is near to the hotel,
I really liked the place,
I wish my family and me never left.

Megan Bratcher (8)
Walton Primary School, Walton

In My Dream World

In my dream world, when I go to sleep,
I see people I've never seen like Harry Potter
And Doctor Who.
I smell the sweet air,
I hear the beautiful sweet birds' song.
I think it would be lovely for it to last,
But once again I wake up
And say goodbye to my dream.

Charlotte Peach (9)
Walton Primary School, Walton

Christmas Time

At Christmas we play fun games,
When it's Christmas it's very exciting,
At Christmas you have lots of lovely food,
Lots of children loudly shouting,
Lots of jokes and tricks,
Lots of children loudly screaming,
Grown-ups shouting and saying no,
In my house it's very noisy.

Lauren Kite (8)
Walton Primary School, Walton

A Holiday In Tenerife

I went on holiday to Tenerife,
I took the whole family to Tenerife,
We had lots of fun at Tenerife,
So much fun at Tenerife,
I swam in the sea at Tenerife,
My dad swam with me at Tenerife,
I swam in a swimming pool every day,
Swim, swim, swim, swim, swim.

Melissa Brandon (8)
Walton Primary School, Walton

Glastonbury Festival

Mud very sticky, deep as a ruler,
Drinks refreshing like an ice pack,
Loud like a person singing to your ear,
Earache at first then it got better,
Singers funny as well as entertaining,
Stages big, huge as can be,
Toilets muddy and smelly, not nice to go in,
Fell over into the mud, very sticky,
Candyfloss sticky, got muddy on the way back,
Waited in the bus then went home.

Thomas Fallows (8)
Walton Primary School, Walton

My Birthday

On my birthday we played kiss chase,
We had lots of yummy food like pizza,
We made up lots of funny jokes,
All of it was a party,
Before it all I was very excited,
It was very noisy,
At the end I was sad that it was over but happy as well
And I can't wait until the next year!

Samuel Chant (8)
Walton Primary School, Walton

Miss Kidd

I met a teacher called Miss Kidd,
She's strict but nice
And very kind,
I wish she never left,
She's fair, kind and helpful,
She's the best teacher yet.

Fiona Shirley (9)
Walton Primary School, Walton

The Witches

Hubble bubble chocolate double,
Cooking up some pots of some trouble.
Into my pot I am going to put
An old mouldy granny's foot.
The three ugly witches laugh and cried
When they decided to make a beehive.
Sticks and stones will break my bones
But spells will never hurt me.
Here's the time, indeed to go,
So please don't forget that mouldy toe.

Chadley Tolliver (11)
Wansdyke Primary School, Whitchurch

Horses

H orses are large, kind and magnificent.
O pen your eyes and enjoy the sight.
R iding is a pleasure, heaven sent.
S o enjoy the power but avoid a fight.
E ven the biggest of horses can be a true gent.
S o be brave, take a chance and ride into the night.

Casey Bardsley (10)
Wansdyke Primary School, Whitchurch

I Wish

I wish I could fly like a bird in the sky.
I wish I could swing like a monkey on a branch.
I wish I was a star in the sky like a fly up high.
I wish I was tall to play netball.
I wish I was high to touch the sky.

Charlie Lenehan (8)
Wansdyke Primary School, Whitchurch

Society

Time to time
> People commit crime
>> Doing things they shouldn't
>>> Along with people that wouldn't

So go away, leave us alone, and don't ring again on your telephone
If you can see someone
> Hiding behind me *say!*

Go away, leave us alone and don't ring again on your telephone
Every time when it's got so hard
> All they know how to do is behave badly

So come here
> *Let us teach you!*

Carlia Zographos (10)
Wansdyke Primary School, Whitchurch

Things

Cars are for driving
Boats are for rowing
Seeds are for growing
Noses for blowing

Dogs are for pawing
Logs are for sawing
Ice is for thawing
Crows are for cawing

Flags are for flying
Stores are for buying
Glasses for spying
Babies for crying

Life is for living.

Callum Matthews (10)
Wansdyke Primary School, Whitchurch

The Four Seasons

Spring is cold as winter,
The beginning of a new year,
The light mornings and dark nights
Reminds me of a new year,
A new beginning.

Summer is as hot as ever
But now here in Bristol it's not as hot
But in Spain and France it's very hot,
As hot as the colour red when you touch it.

Autumn, autumn getting colder,
Still quite hot but not as warm,
The lovely days of crisp leaves falling,
Changing colours every season.

Winter, winter freezing cold,
A time for big coats, gloves, hats and scarves,
On Christmas Day the snow is falling,
Snowball fights and snowmen to build.

Sophie Shaw (8)
Wansdyke Primary School, Whitchurch

I Wish

I wish I was a bird in the sky flying with the planes.
I wish I was a champion at skiing and snowboarding.
I wish I could buy things without paying.
I wish I was in a comic or on a TV show.
I wish I was a writer who writes poems all day long.
I wish I had the newest technology like a robot.
I wish I was a Cyberman or a Dalek.

Thomas Shorland (8)
Wansdyke Primary School, Whitchurch

My Large Sunflower

On Thursday afternoon I planted a sunflower seed
And I wanted to water it, I wanted to feed it,
Two days passed and it still didn't grow *at all!*

Three days passed
And at last,
I saw a tiny stem
And then, and then . . .
Two little leaves
Smiling at me,
It's such a sweet thing to see.

One week later my sunflower
Was 1m high!
The biggest flower,
I've ever seen, so tall, in one week!

Three months passed and my sunflower,
The world's biggest flower
Touched the clouds!
It sounds,
To be impossible,
But it was true
And I hadn't anything to do.

Sometimes, when I'm late for school,
I climb up my large sunflower,
Call my bird
And fly to school . . .
When I want to come back,
I call again
My bird plane,
Fly back home
And everything's done . . .

Paula Pomothy (11)
Wansdyke Primary School, Whitchurch

I Wish I Had A Puppy

I wish I had a puppy
One small and cute
Tiny and sweet
But bigger than a newt

I would play with her every day
And take her to the park
Play lots of games
But never in the dark

We could always play fetch
And chase the ball
Do lots of running
And try not to fall

If my puppy was unwell
I would take her to the vet
Then she will be OK
And be my cute pet

I could take her to school
And put her in my backpack
Play with her every lunchtime
But not to eat my snack

I could call her Lucky
Or call her Fluffy
Or even call her Cuddles
Oh I wish I had a puppy.

Chelsea Harrison (10)
Wansdyke Primary School, Whitchurch

Missing Home

Children whining,
Mothers pining
As their men go to war.

Sirens wailing,
Bomb blast trailing,
The country can't take anymore.

Soldiers crying,
Soldiers lying
In the cold muddy trenches.

Fear in their eyes
Beneath the smoky skies
As they lay in death's clenches.

So let's all remember,
Let's not forget
Or the next world war will be the worst one yet!

Dan Bartley (11)
Wansdyke Primary School, Whitchurch

Autumn

In autumn there are wicked winds
That give you colds,
Bustling noises coming from bare branches, that sound like *ooh, ooh.*
Children inside playing games and drinking hot chocolate,
Buying warmer clothes,
Going to bed early, wearing bed socks,
Having extra quilts to keep you snug as a bug,
The days are getting shorter,
Nights are getting so much longer,
The days are getting colder, colder, colder winter.

Molly Selby (10)
Wansdyke Primary School, Whitchurch

The Comparing Poem

The keeper is an octopus
With eight arms,
Saving every shot.

The defenders are walruses
Big and *strong,*
Stopping every shot.

The midfielders are salmons
Darting down the line,
Crossing and shooting.

The strikers are sharks
Hungry for the ball,
Scoring and celebrating.

Tom Martin (10)
Wansdyke Primary School, Whitchurch

Football

Football is fun
I like to run
My team is cool
We so totally rule
I score when I can
I am the man
I am also glad
Because my coach is my friend's dad
He is really mad
It's fun when we win
When does my next match begin?

James Ford
Wansdyke Primary School, Whitchurch

My Snoring Sister

The bright light from the TV shone around the room,
Lying on the sofa, one eye opened the other half closed.
'Time for bed everyone,' said Dad, 'come on girls, let's go.'
'You will never get up for school, never will. No, no!'

Splash, gargle, splosh, this toothpaste is so very minty hot.
All the clothes folded and pressed, shoes and slippers placed tidy.
Sleep is good for the mind or so I am told, silence not even the drop of
a pin.
Jump into bed and read a story, then I will tuck you in.

The room is dark, the curtains are closed,
Leave the landing light on just in case.
A whistling noise can clearly be heard, is a storm heading
towards us?
Thundering, rumbling, rattling could it be a double-decker bus?

Loud then quiet, loud then quiet, loud then quiet,
What on Earth could be making all that noise?
What type of animal or monster could create that sound?
Creature of the night, fox, badger or hound?

A wheezy, chesty, growling din,
There is no let up, it's getting louder and louder.
Snarling, snorting, oh no surely not, it cannot be this,
Yes it's coming from next door, it's my snoring little sis!

Aimee Coombs (10)
Wansdyke Primary School, Whitchurch

Moving House

Today we are moving house, it seems a lot of bother.
I woke up in my room and will be sleeping in another.
I'm glad the new pink room is for my little brother,
Mum has been fussing for weeks over our new address.
I can't see what all the worry is about, for me there is no stress.

Zachary Smith (10)
Wansdyke Primary School, Whitchurch

The Skateboard Kid

Hi, I'm the skateboard kid
And when you take off the lid
You get amazement from the skateboard kid.
I'm the best, a lot better than the rest,
Even Chad Muska,
A so called huska
Cos . . .
I'm the skateboard kid
And when you take off the lid
You get amazement from the skateboard kid.
Now here's me doing a trick
Known as a kick flip
And I'm the skateboard kid
And when you take off the lid
You get amazement from the . . .
Skateboard kid!

Ryan Spillane (11)
Wansdyke Primary School, Whitchurch

Slavery

Slavery is hurtful,
It kills people inside.
Whips, canes
Coming towards
The little slave

As he cries
The painful words,
'Ouch, why are you doing this?'
Child you won't understand.
They will never understand,
How did he get through this?

So my message is stop slavery!

Kelsie Davis (10)
Wansdyke Primary School, Whitchurch

My Pot

Into my pot
There now must go
An old musty tongue
And a person's lungs

A revolting bum
And a rotting gum
Kangaroo's guts
And a body with cuts

Hubble bubble at the double
Cooking pot stir up some trouble
Some blood on a king
Who wears bling, bling
A massive bogey

Hubble bubble at the cooking pot
Stir up some trouble
Bat's fangs
And some cans
Hubble bubble at the double
Cooking pot stir up some trouble.

Ermes Musumeci (10)
Wansdyke Primary School, Whitchurch

The Willow

There's a willow right outside the window
The wind blows its beauty to the left and to the right.
The bright green leaves flow with the wind.
The squirrels climb it and birds rest in it but they always leave
But what never leaves is its beauty.

Callum Lacey (10)
Wansdyke Primary School, Whitchurch

Fair Trade

They work all day,
They work all night,
They can't complain
Or put up a fight.

Stole upon the twilight hour,
Striving for life,
But lost to power.

Endless hours working in the heat,
Paid a pittance,
Given blistering feet.

Cadbury, Nestlé, Mars that you eat,
Are given to you, you don't take as a treat,
Try something different, give your taste buds a new,
Buy fair-traded chocolate and give them a life too.

Abigail Underhill (11)
Wansdyke Primary School, Whitchurch

Christmas

Christmas, the 25th, happy day whatever you want to call it,
Everyone shall celebrate but some shall not.
But for ones who do, merry Christmas,
Presents, snow, fun and food,
All this happens on one special day.
But make sure you do have fun because it only comes once a year,
But remember the true meaning of it, the birth of Jesus Christ.

Josh Fry (10)
Wansdyke Primary School, Whitchurch

Sense Poem

I can hear the cold breeze tickling my arms.
Now I can hear the rustle of trees swaying in the wind.

I can see the butterflies and bees carrying nectar from flower
to flower.
Now I can see children playing and laughing.

I can smell the fresh air as it comes towards me.
Now I can smell the sweet smelling flowers.

I can taste the air.
Now I can taste the sweet orange as I pop it in my mouth.

I can feel the pebbly ground.
Now I can feel the bumpy hard bark on the tall green trees.

Sophie Bennett (9)
Wansdyke Primary School, Whitchurch

Hubble Bubble

Hubble bubble at the double
Cooking pot stir up some trouble

Into my pot there must go
Greasy grow
And a slimy toe

A swarm of flies
A wily whale
Five dead ants
And a broken scale

Hubble bubble at the double
Cooking pot stir up some trouble.

Michael Bray (10)
Wansdyke Primary School, Whitchurch

I Wish

I wish I had a pet polar bear,
I wish I had a year's supply of food,
I wish I could be an eagle soaring through the sky,
I wish I could be a fish zooming through the sea,
I wish I could be a penguin skillfully dodging leopard seals to and fro,
I wish I was a dog digging energetically,
I wish I could be a monkey swinging acrobatically,
I wish there were four wheeled bicycles,
I wish that I had rocket shoes so I can fly through the sky,
I wish that Bristol City were number one in the Championship.
If only that would be true my life would be complete.

Josh Bennett (9)
Wansdyke Primary School, Whitchurch

Christmas Poem

It's getting cold,
It's time to hold
Each other's hands
And listen to carol bands,
There's no time to delay . . .
It's nearly Christmas Day!
On that day there's Christmas presents,
On that day we must open presents just . . .
To have some fun!
I can feel the wetness coming through my boots,
The traffic on the road, all cars hoot!

Georgia Mae Davies (9)
Wansdyke Primary School, Whitchurch

Season Poem

Winter is here
So everyone cheer.

Christmas is coming
Let's do some running.

It's Christmas Day
Let's say hey.

Spring is here
Let's all cheer.

It is so sunny
Let's go get some money.

It is autumn
Let's all see the leaves falling.

It is autumn time
Let's see the leaves fall and see the different coloured leaves.

It's autumn
The leaves are falling everywhere
Let's rake up the leaves in piles.

Summer's here, let's cheer
So wear summer clothes.

Summer's here, let's cheer
Let's go swimming.

Abby Louise Bray (9)
Wansdyke Primary School, Whitchurch

Winter

As the snow comes in from the north west
I can see icicles dropping down like rain,
The snowflakes dance in the sky and snow on the top of trees.

The snow is finally here, more and more snowflakes are dancing
in the sky,

The moment is here at last,
Presents are here from Santa of course,
Stockings are full, presents are being wrapped.

Let's put on your scarves, your gloves and hat,
Chuck on your coat, go outside, make a snowman and that's that.

Abbie Iles (8)
Wansdyke Primary School, Whitchurch

Autumn Time

Leaves falling to the ground,
They come in reds and lots of brown.
People collect all the leaves,
While autumn has its breeze.
I go out and have some fun
While autumn is nearly done!

It's summertime, people are out in the sun,
Having a handful of fun.
People are going swimming in the pool,
But people are not going to school!

Lauren Davies (9)
Wansdyke Primary School, Whitchurch

Spring

Spring is a time where the flowers bloom,
Where the birds sing and where the lambs leap,
Frolic through the flowers with friends, give them perfume,
Flowers to give pictures to draw,
Bunnies hopping,
Vegetables fresh for wrapping.

Chloe Boyes (8)
Wansdyke Primary School, Whitchurch

In 1066

In 1066 they were fighting with sticks
And crashing around on the floor.

Many men died and women cried
And mourned for evermore.

That was 1066.

Thomas Stone (10)
Wansdyke Primary School, Whitchurch

I Wish

I wish I was Elvis and made millions of people happy.
I wish I could swing like a monkey.
I wish I could soar like an eagle
And I wish I could be a fly up high in the sky.
But I'd rather be me than anything else!

Callum Phillips (9)
Wansdyke Primary School, Whitchurch

My Birthday

My birthday's coming up
I really want a pup
Pens and pencils are so cool
I also want a football
Cards and signs fill up the wall
Let's go shopping to the mall
Birthday presents everywhere
My mum has bought me a teddy bear
Let's go to sleep for tomorrow is my birthday
The day is here
It's time to cheer
Because it's present time
Yaaaaaay!

Stephanie Louise Reid (8)
Wansdyke Primary School, Whitchurch

My Room Poem

My room is the best
My room is good for a rest
My room is really great
And I always invite my mates
When my brother comes in
He always messes it up
So I have to clean it up
When my mum comes in
She always changes my stuff around
And I have to put it back
When my dad comes in
He always takes my stuff.

Oliver Pace (8)
Wansdyke Primary School, Whitchurch

Young Writers Information

We hope you have enjoyed reading this book - and that you will continue to enjoy it in the coming years.

If you like reading and writing poetry drop us a line, or give us a call, and we'll send you a free information pack.

Alternatively if you would like to order further copies of this book or any of our other titles, then please give us a call or log onto our website at www.youngwriters.co.uk

**Young Writers Information
Remus House
Coltsfoot Drive
Peterborough
PE2 9JX**

(01733) 890066